SINGAPORE
500 Early Postcards

This book is dedicated to the memory of my parents
Mr. Cheah Kim Yeam
(1904–1987)
and
Madam Ooi Gaik Phuan
(1907–1992)

First published in 2006
EDITIONS DIDIER MILLET
121 Telok Ayer Street, #03-01,
Singapore 068590

Reprinted in 2008

www.edmbooks.com

Editorial Director
TIMOTHY AUGER

Editor
GREGORY LEE

Designer
LISA DAMAYANTI

Production Manager
SIN KAM CHEONG

Colour Separation by
COLOURSCAN CO. PTE LTD

Printed in Singapore by
STAR STANDARD INDUSTRIES PTE LTD

Overall design © Editions Didier Millet 2006
Images © Cheah Jin Seng 2006

Typeset in Garamond on Exel Bulky (Satin) paper.

ISBN: 978-981-4155-66-3

Front cover: ORCHARD ROAD, SINGAPORE. (C 1930)
Divided-back
Publisher: M.W.P., Singapore

Back cover: CHINESE GIRL. (C 1900)
Divided-back
Publisher: Max H. Hilckes, Singapore

SINGAPORE
500 Early Postcards

Cheah Jin Seng

EDITIONS DIDIER MILLET

North Boat Quay, Singapore.

Orchard Road, Singapore.

Collyer Quay, Singapore.

An Overview

Early History of Picture Postcards of Singapore

The Collection:

SUNNY SINGAPORE

A SERIES OF 38 PHOTOGRAVURE
VIEWS IN SEPIA TONE

KELLY & WALSH LD.
SINGAPORE   SHANGHAI   HONGKONG

The earliest known of any postcards are the private cards in the United States known as the "Lipman's Postal Card" that were printed in 1861. Austria is credited with the production of the first official (governmental) postcard in 1869, following the proposal put forward by Dr. Heinrich von Stephan, the director of its postal service, in 1865.[1] This was followed subsequently by England producing the first picture postcard (ppc) in 1894.[1] By the end of the 19th century, picture postcards (ppcs) were produced almost worldwide.

The craze for collecting ppcs began in the 1890s and it is even said that Queen Victoria had been an avid collector of ppc! Interestingly, people who collect ppcs are referred to differently in different countries; a ppcs collector is known as a cartologist in England, a deltiologist in America and a cartophilist in France!

Several books on ppcs and historical photographs of Singapore have already been published locally: "Singapore 1870s–1940s in Pictures", a bilingual book published by the Ministry of Culture, Singapore, in 1980[2]; "Singapore in Pictures, 1819–1945", published by the *Sin Chew Jit Poh*, a Singapore Chinese news daily, and the Ministry of Culture in 1981[3]; "Singapore Retrospect Through Postcards: 1900–1930"[4]; "Singapore Historical Postcards, From the National Archives Collection"[5]; "Passing Through Singapore, 1900–1930" by Jean-Pierre Mialaret in 1986[6] and "Reminiscences of the Straits Settlements Through Postcards" published in 2005 by the National Archives of Malaysia and the National Archives of Singapore[7].

Two earlier books that utilise a mixture of ppcs and historical photographs are also worthy of mention: "Character of Light – a guide to the buildings of Singapore" by Marjorie Doggett in 1957[8] and "Singapore: Then and Now" by Ray Tyres in two volumes in 1976[9].

This book is modelled upon an earlier publication, "Indonesia: 500 Early Postcards" by Leo Haks and Steven Wachlin[10]. This present book attempts to improve on the above-mentioned earlier publications, having the advantage of hindsight and improved technology. For example, the ppcs are shown in their actual sizes and in colour, while many ppcs in this book are seldom seen and many others have not been published previously.

The advent of the Internet and online auctions (such as *EBay.com*) in the past decade have allowed ppc collectors to view and acquire many uncommon ppcs of Singapore. However, no collection of ppcs can be ever complete, but that is the beauty of the hobby of cartology.

I have handed to the publishers a mess of manuscripts and ppcs; that the finished product is a work of art pleasing to behold and read is due to the tremendous hard work of the publishers. Should readers find in this book something pleasing to read and gloss over, then my labours and that of the publishers would not have been in vain!

Above: RAFFLES HOTEL, SINGAPORE. (C 1935)
Back: Divided
Publisher: Koh & Co., Singapore

Opposite: The front cover of a picture postcard booklet entitled "Sunny Singapore".

Publisher: Kelly & Walsh Ltd, Singapore, Shanghai, Hongkong
A bustling street scene at Raffles Square, Singapore, around 1935.

EARLY HISTORY of PICTURE POSTCARDS of SINGAPORE

The front of the first-ever postal stationery postcard issued in the Straits Settlements. It was issued in 1879.
(*See* [3A])

The reverse side of the above shown postcard. It was sent from John Little & Co. Ltd, Singapore, to Raja Brooke of Sarawak.
(*See* [3B])

Origin of the Picture Postcard

There are two types of postcards (pc): the postal stationery postcard (pspc) and picture postcard (ppc). Following the introduction of the first official postcard by Austria in 1869[1], the Straits Settlements (S.S.) (comprising Singapore, Malacca and Penang) introduced the first postcard in 1879. A 3¢ carmine pspc issued in 1893 and used in 1903 is shown with the front of the card having the printed 3¢ carmine stamp of Queen Victoria and the words "POST/ROYAL COAT OF ARMS/CARD" with space for the address below [3A (*left, top*)]; the back of the pspc is reserved for writing the message [3B (*left, middle*)].

The first ppc of Singapore in the author's collection was sent from Singapore to Germany on 14 September 1895; it was a German ppc printed in colour of a sailing steamship [1].

An early pspc was sent on 15 September 1897 to Austria. It had a picture in black and white printed on the reverse: the scene shows a steamer with the coastline and Fort Canning behind it; the front of the ppc is shown in [2].

Picture postcards were introduced in 1870 in Europe by Germany, France, Switzerland and England. They were to be followed by Belgium, Holland and Canada (1871), Russia (1872) and, Spain and Japan (1873). On 1 September 1894, Britain allowed privately printed ppcs to be produced for use with adhesive postage stamps and the first issue of British private ppcs was issued in 1894. The Universal Postal Union (UPU) accepted private postcards on 23 January 1896, with a maximum size of 5.5 x 3.5 inches and the word "Postcard" printed on the reverse (address) side.

Undivided-Back; Divided-Back and Postal Rates

Under UPU regulations, the address side of the postcard was reserved for the sticking of the postage stamp, the writing of the name of the addressee and its destination address. This gives rise to the description "Undivided-Back" ppc, a format that has no central vertical line to divide the spaces for the address and destination. The obverse side (picture or view side) has either a picture or multiple vignettes, occupying a portion with the remaining empty space for the message to be written. However, ppc with the Undivided-Back format has limited space for the message. One of the earliest Undivided-Back ppcs with an adhesive postage stamp in this collection was sent from Singapore on 18 June 1898 to Germany [5; 6].

In June 1906, the UPU accepted both official and privately issued postcards with the Divided-Back (where one could write the message on the same side as the address). The postcard had to have the wordings "UNION POSTALE UNIVERSELLE" printed on its address sides; the Straits Settlements (S.S.), being a member of UPU, had to comply with the UPU regulations. The 1906 S.S. Postal Department Annual Report by W.G. Bell, the acting Postmaster, also stated that "The regulations with regard to postcards were modified during the year so as to admit cards bearing communications on the left hand half of the address side at postcard rate and private cards bearing the inscription "POSTCARD"[11] were allowed to pass at the rate for printed matter provided they were otherwise in conformity with regulations." This report confirms 1906 as being the year Divided-Back ppcs were officially accepted for usage in the S.S. The printed matter regulation also allowed private ppcs to be posted as printed matter for 1¢ postage to anywhere in the world – as long as the weight did not exceed 2 ounces (57 grams). This regulation contributed tremendously to the popularity in the use of the ppcs.[11,12]

Although the Divided-Back [4 (*right, top*)] format of ppcs was introduced in 1906; the Undivided-Back [5 (*right, middle*)] ppcs continued to be sold and used well after 1906, as publishers had considerable stocks of the Undivided-Back ppcs.[11]

Postal rates varied according to the destination and period. For sending within the S.S. and Federated Malay States, the rate started at 1¢ in 1899 and rose to 4¢ in 1941. For the rest of the world, the rate started from 3¢ to 8¢ during these periods. During the 1900s, the printed matter rate was considered a much cheaper way to send postcards. Hence many used ppcs are found with the word "POSTCARD" deleted and replaced by "PRINTED MATTER", "PRINTED PAPER" or even "BOOK POST". With the advent of regular air services in the 1930s, special airmail rates for postcards were introduced but as they were expensive, they were not frequently used.[13]

The Rise of the Picture Postcard Trade

When the picture postcard (ppc) was first introduced in Singapore in 1897, its sale was infrequent due to the high cost of the ppc and postage. The early history of Singapore's privately printed ppcs has been traced by Chris Mortimer.[14, 15] It is estimated that between 500,000 - 550,000 ppcs were dispatched (i.e. postally used) from the Straits Settlements over the period 1898–1901, with a large proportion of cards originating from Singapore. In addition, a large number of ppcs would have been published but not posted; some were leftovers while others were sold to collectors. The rapid growth of postal business necessitated the opening of three sub-post offices in Singapore in 1897 at Kandang Kerbau, Tanglin and Tanjong Pagar.[14] In the 1905 S.S. Annual

Report, N. Trotter (Postmaster-General) wrote: "The popularity of pictorial postcards is responsible for an extraordinary increase in this labour-saving method of complimentary communication". In the 1906 S.S. Annual Report, W.G. Bell (the acting Postmaster-General) wrote: "The most notable increase is in the number of postcards and is attributable, no doubt, to the vogue of the picture postcard and to the increased use of the postcard for advertising."[14]

Throughout the world (Europe, Britain, USA as well as in Singapore), the period 1906–1913 is considered the boom period of ppcs and is often dubbed "The Golden Era of Picture Postcards"[1] or "The Golden Era of Singapore Picture Postcards"[16]. "The Golden Era of Singapore Picture Postcards" had come about due to various factors: the opening of the Suez Canal in 1869 led more travellers to Singapore; the advent of cheap privately printed ppcs; the introduction of the Divided-Back ppc and inexpensive postal rates for such cards in 1905. The "Golden Era" ended in August 1914 with the outbreak of the First World War (1914–1918).

The Colour of the Pictures

The first ppc of Singapore was produced in 1897 by the photographic firm of G.R. Lambert (*right, bottom*) in Singapore: a 3¢ carmine Queen Victoria printed postal stationery postcard (issued in 1893 by the Government Postal Department) was used with a thin real photograph in black and white layered on the obverse blank side of the postcard. The photograph did not cover the whole of the card; one can feel the thickness of the photograph on the sides and bottom of the picture [7].

The early photographs in black and white layered on postal stationery postcard were expensive; after the First World War (1914–1918) to the Second World War (1941–1945), black and white real photographic ppc were mass produced privately, as it was cheaper due to the advance in photographic technology. [9] shows a

The address side of a postcard showing the Divided-Back format. (*See* [4])

The address side of a postcard showing the Undivided-Back format. (*See* [5])

A photograph of G.R. Lambert taken in 1894.

A hand-tinted postcard showing soldiers marching from Cavenagh Bridge, the Old Chinese Temple and New Year sports. (*See* [17])

Beach Road (c 1910), showing the Hippodrome and Alhambra theatres on the right hand side. (*See* [21])

A label from Nakajima & Co.

typical black and white real photographic ppc that is dated 1922.

The majority of the ppcs of Singapore are photographs. Most of the monochrome ppcs are in black and white; other colours that are occasionally encountered are in orange [11], sepia/brown [12], blue/azure [14] or green [15].

When the photographers produced the ppcs around 1900, they were in black and white [16; 18]; at a later stage, the same photographers had coloured them [17 (*left, top*); 19]. From 1905, coloured ppcs were common, and most coloured ppcs are made from photographs; occasionally they are produced from artists' paintings.

The Photographers

The picture postcard is a product of photography and the history of ppc closely follows the advancement in photographic technology. Many of the early ppc publishers were professional photographers, having established photo studios in Singapore. Although the earliest photographic views of Singapore were taken in 1844[17] by Jules Itier; it was G.R. Lambert (a German national from Dresden) whose arrival in Singapore in 1867 was to have the most significant impact on the history of ppc in Singapore. Lambert opened his photographic studio in 1875 but he left Singapore in 1885, and from 1885–1905, the firm was managed by another German, Alexander Koch. From 1905, the firm was managed by H.T. Jansen[18], who was also German. Koch and Jensen should have been the ones credited for the ppcs of Singapore published by the firm of G.R. Lambert, but this fact is seldom mentioned. The firm finally wound up in 1918.[17]

From 1897 to 1914, German photographers operated most of the photographic studios in Singapore. This was not surprising as Germany was the leader in the early development of photography.

Besides G.R. Lambert, other Germans also set up photographic studios in Singapore (e.g. George S. Michael, Wilson & Co., N & J Thomson, Schuren and A. Schleesselmann[17]).

The German photographers left Singapore from 1914 to 1918 during the First World War; this was compounded by the Indian (Sepoy) Mutiny in 1915 when the Germans sided with the Indian Mutineers. They were gradually replaced by Chinese and Japanese photographers. The Chinese photographic shops included Quan Seng (62 North Bridge Road), Pun Lun (13 High Street), Lee Brothers and Kong Hing Chiong & Co. (104 North Bridge Road). Nakajima & Co. (91 and 92 Bras Basah Road), S.T. Yama (junction of Hylam Street and Middle Road) and Togo & Co. were well known Japanese photographers. Picture postcards from Nakajima & Co. are common while those produced by a Chinese photographic studio are rare [21 (*left, middle*)].

The Publishers

Two of the most well known publishers of ppcs in Singapore were Ribeiro and Co. and Koh & Co.

Ribeiro & Co.

"Civility to customers and reasonable prices are foundations upon which the success of many business has been built, among them that of Messrs C.A. Ribeiro & Co. [*opposite page, right, top*)], of Singapore. Although established only about 16 years ago, they were now in the front rank of Singapore stationers, printers and book binders. The firm commenced business in Malacca Street solely as philatelists, and in this line, they speedily acquired a high reputation among stamp collectors. At the end of five years, they entered into the general stationery and rubber stamp business, and soon afterwards, moved into more extensive premises in Raffles Place next to Robinsons. There, at the request of numbers of their constituents, they added printing and book binding departments, and these were attended by such success that in 1901, it was found necessary to acquire more plants. Two years later, it became so difficult to cope with the increasing work that the stamp business was given up in order that the firm might concentrate on the printing and stationery departments. The last named is replete with every description of stationery, and it is now proposed to purchase new printing plants."[18]

Koh & Co.

Koh & Co. published numerous beautiful and colourful ppcs of Singapore; it was founded in 1905 by Koh Hoon Teck, a Singapore-born Chinese.[18] It published a "Postcard Exchange Register", as a monthly photographic magazine; these magazines contained a wealth of information of interest to ppcs collectors. 14 of these monthly magazines published in 1908 and 1909 were examined and while the 1908 issues were found to be designated Vol. II, the 1909 issues were labelled Vol. III. This indicates that the publication was most probably started in 1907. However, it is not known when this publication ceased.

An issue (October 1908) of Koh & Co.'s "Postcard Exchange Register" (*right, bottom*) shows Boat Quay on its cover in 1908.[19] This issue has 28 pages; on page 18 is a photograph of the premises of Koh & Co. (*right, second from bottom*).

In the June 1909 issue of Koh & Co.'s "Postcard Exchange Register" lies a photograph of Koh Hoon Teck alias H.T. Koh, proprietor of Koh & Co.[20] (*right, second from top*). In it was also announced the winners of a Postcard Exhibition held in Singapore a few months earlier in February: "Our Postcard Exhibition was held on the 4th, 5th and 6th instants... On the 3rd instant, Mr. H.T. Jensen of Messrs, Lambert & Co. and Mr. Lee King Yan of Chop Koon Sun acted as judges... Mr. Lee Kim San, Singapore, was awarded a silver medal with a gold centre piece, and an album, for a collection which while

being excellent, embraced the widest variety. Miss Daphne Richards, Singapore, came second... Mr. Chin Tiong Kim, Singapore, was awarded the third prize..."[21]

Koh & Co. was located at 90 Bras Basah Road (Raffles Hotel Building) and they doubled up as book sellers, stationers or even drapers.[18] Tourists would find a good selection of picture postcards and postcard albums, and uncommon stamps.[18]

Other Publishers

It is often difficult to distinguish publishers from printers, stationers or retailers, and thus these terms are often used interchangeably. Understandably, as many of the early postcards were produced in Europe, numerous Singapore ppcs were printed in England; some were printed in Germany, Russia and Japan. Many Singapore publishers such as Kelly & Walsh, Methodist Publishing House, the Continental Stamp Co., Straits Times Press, John Little, Co-operative Agency S.S. and M. Yahaya sold ppcs too. Unfortunately, there are also a large number of ppcs with no mention of any publisher and some are embossed with just an emblem (such as an Eagle).

Curiously, some Singapore ppcs have been found to be printed in foreign countries (apparently for use in those countries) [22].

Japanese Invasion of Singapore

Between the two World Wars, the ppc trade in Singapore surged due to the advance in photographic technology; the rise in the real photographic ppcs in black and white was conspicuous. Prior to the Japanese Invasion of Singapore on 8 February 1942, most of the ppcs sent from Singapore were by military personnel. With the Japanese Occupation of Singapore (at a time when Singapore was known as Syonanto), a chapter in the history of Singapore ppcs was ended. One of the last ppcs to be sent before the capitulation of Singapore was on 5 June 1941 [23].

C.A. Ribeiro & Co. Establishment (c 1908) (from *20th Century Impressions of British Malaya*).

Portrait of Koh Hoon Teck alias H.T. Koh, proprietor of Koh & Co.

The premise of Koh & Co.'s (c 1908).

Front cover of Koh & Co.'s "Postcard Exchange Register", October 1908

A road (possibly Orchard Road) at the end of the 19th century; it is well-shaded by tall trees on either side. (*See* [24])

A picturesque scene of the Hotel de l'Europe amidst bright orange flame-of-the-forest trees. (*See* [44])

Right: Advertisements printed on the back of photographs advertising the services of photographers G.R. Lambert & Co. and A. Schleesselmann.

The First Picture Postcards of Singapore

The first picture postcards (ppcs) of Singapore were produced in 1897 using the official Straits Settlements (S.S.) Queen Victoria 3¢ carmine postal stationery (ps) postcard (issued in 1893). The blank message side of the postal stationery postcard was initially layered with a thin black and white photograph [2] or later printed with a picture (in black and white or colour). Thus, the first ppc was made from a postal stationery postcard (pspc); an appropriate term for it would be postal stationery picture postcard (psppc).

Judging from the earliest and latest postmarks on these psppcs, these were produced from 1897 to 1902. They are rare and are much sought-after by collectors.

The firm of G.R. Lambert at Gresham House, Battery Road in 1908, produced most of these psppcs; the evidence for this is that some of the photographs on these psppcs exist with the embossed logo of the Company and some of the photographs and pictures were reused in later ppcs bearing the Company's imprint. At least one of those psppcs is produced by Max H. Hilckes, Singapore.

G.R. Lambert & Co. was not only famous in Singapore, it was also appointed photographers to H.M., the King of Siam and H.R.H., the Sultan of Johore: this is proudly printed on the back of a photograph taken in Singapore in 1894.

"Messrs Lambert has maintained a high reputation for artistic portraiture, and of landscapes they have are of the finest collections in the East, comprising about three thousand subjects relating to Siam, Singapore, Borneo, Malaya and China. An extensive trade is done in picture postcards, the turnover being about a quarter of a million cards a year. A large stock of apparatus for amateurs is always kept on hand. Messrs Lambert & Co.'s head office is at Gresham House, Battery Road, and they have branch studios in Orchard Road and at Kuala Lumpur."[18]

The first postal stationery picture postcard (psppc) of Singapore is listed in Higgins & Gage (1971)[22] as No. 13a (3¢ carmine on buff postcard with two multi colour pictures and "Greetings from Singapore" on its back; no date of issue was stated). Wong Han Min (1995) illustrated four examples of these psppc.[23] A simple approach to classify these psppcs is to classify them according to the picture on the back (message side). The pictures may be grouped under three main types:

(A) Real photographs in black and white.
  [7; 24-40]
(B) Printed pictures in black and white.
  [2; 41-42]
(C) Printed pictures in colour.
  [43-49]

The message (blank) side of the postcard had a thin black and white photograph gummed on it (Type A); a black and white picture printed on it (Type B) or a coloured picture printed on it (Type C). As these ppcs were made from postal stationery postcards, they should be called postal stationery postcards (psppcs) to distinguish them from ordinary privately printed picture postcards (ppcs) where postage stamps had to be affixed.

[1]

Untitled

Cancellation: 1895

This picture postcard shows a picture postcard of a
German steamship on top, and the written message
below; it is likely to be the first picture postcard sent
from Singapore.

[2]

GREETING FROM SINGAPORE.

Cancellation: 1897
Publisher: Not stated. Attributed to G.R. Lambert & Co.,
Singapore

Among the first picture postcards of Singapore; it was
sent to Austria on 15 September 1897.

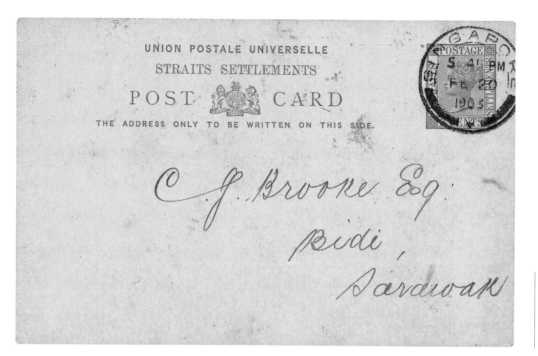

[3A]
Untitled

Cancellation: 1903
Publisher: Thomas De La Rue Co., London

The front view of a Straits Settlements 3¢ carmine
Queen Victoria postal stationery postcard (issued
in 1893 and sent from Singapore to Sarawak).

[3B]
Untitled

Cancellation: 1903

Shows the written message on the reverse side of
[3A]. It was sent from John Little & Co. Ltd,
Singapore, to Raja Brooke of Sarawak.

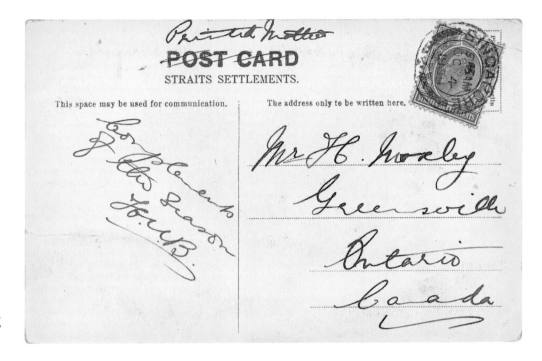

[4]
Untitled [A Divided-Back postcard].

Cancellation: 1909

A picture postcard with the Divided-Back format. A 1¢ King Edward VII stamp is affixed at the top right hand corner, and it was sent from Singapore to Canada.

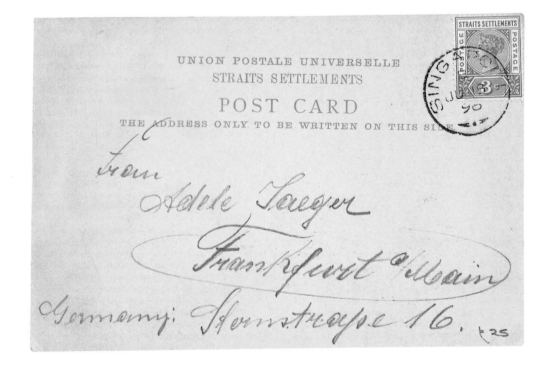

[5]
Untitled [An Undivided-Back postcard].

Cancellation: 1898

A picture postcard with the Undivided-Back format. A 3¢ Straits Settlements stamp can be seen at the top right hand corner.

[6]
GREETINGS FROM SINGAPORE.

Cancellation: 1898
Publisher: Not stated. Attributed to G.R. Lambert & Co., Singapore

This postcard shows a number of vignettes depicting black and white photographs of a rickshaw, Collyer Quay, Cavenagh Bridge, etc.

[7]
Untitled [Indian Snake Charmers].

Cancellation: 1901
Back: Undivided
Publisher: Not stated. Attributed to G.R. Lambert & Co., Singapore

A photographic picture postcard showing two Indian Snake Charmers.

[8]
AMERICAN FLOATING DOCK, "DEWEY", SINGAPORE.

Cancellation: 1909
Back: Divided

[9]
SINGAPORE RIVER, SINGAPORE.

Cancellation: 1922
Back: Divided

This is a real black and white picture postcard showing the Singapore River in the 1900s.

Victoria Memorial Hall, Singapore

[10]

BOAT QUAY, CHINESE QUARTER. SINGAPORE. (1910)

Cancellation: 1910
Back: Undivided
Publisher: Whiteaway Laidlaw & Co., Singapore, Penang, Ipoh and Kuala Lumpur

The Chinese Quarters at Boat Quay; a black and white ink-sketched picture postcard.

[11]

VICTORIA MEMORIAL HALL, SINGAPORE. (c 1920)

Back: Divided

An unusual picture postcard in a deep orange shade, showing the Victoria Memorial Hall, Singapore.

H 278   Orchard Road, Singapore.

[12]

ORCHARD ROAD, SINGAPORE. (C 1915)

Back: Divided
Series and/or No.: H 278
Publisher: Japanese

A sepia-toned picture postcard showing Orchard Road around 1915. The message at the back reads: "This is a good picture of the main road to the town of Singapore. You will see the rickshaws, bullock carts and road sweepers".

Singapore. Battery Road.

[13]

SINGAPORE, BATTERY ROAD.

Cancellation: 1908
Back: Undivided

This is a coloured picture postcard that was sent from Singapore to Italy in 1908.

[14]

GREETINGS FROM SINGAPORE.

Cancellation: 1900
Back: Undivided
Series and/or No.: 5
Publisher: C.A. Ribeiro & Co., Singapore

This is a triview postcard in azure showing three vignettes of the "Impounding Reservoir[s]" of Bukit Timah and McRitchie, and the "Race Course" (at Race Course Road).

[15]

GREETING FROM SINGAPORE. (C 1900)

Back: Undivided
Series and/or No.: 59070
Publisher/Photographer: Max Ludwig, Deutsche Burchandlung, Singapore – Hong Kong

Presenting a green-toned picture postcard of four views (Botanic Gardens, Post Office, Johnston's Pier, Government Office).

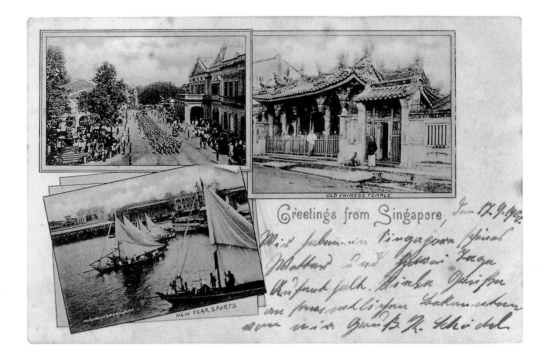

[16]

GREETINGS FROM SINGAPORE.

Cancellation: 1900
Back: Undivided
Publisher: Not stated. Attributed to G.R. Lambert & Co., Singapore

A triview black and white picture postcard with three vignettes of soldiers marching from Cavenagh Bridge; the Old Chinese Temple and New Year Sports.

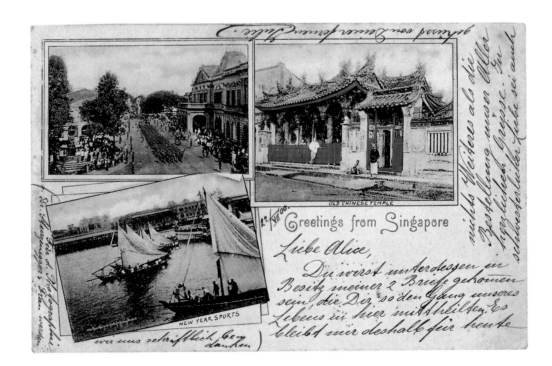

[17]

GREETINGS FROM SINGAPORE.

Cancellation: 1890
Back: Undivided

Similar to **[16]**, but hand-tinted in colour, this postcard was sent from Singapore to Germany.

[18]
GREETINGS FROM SINGAPORE.

Cancellation: 1898
Back: Undivided
Publisher: Not stated. Attributed to G.R. Lambert
& Co., Singapore

This biview black and white postcard shows a
Malay lady and the "Malay Craft Harbour".

[19]
GREETINGS FROM SINGAPORE.

Cancellation: 1899
Back: Undivided

Similar to [18] but this postcard is hand-tinted in
colour.

[20]
SINGAPORE GOVERNMENT HOUSE. (C 1905)

Back: Undivided

Made from an artist's watercolour painting, this coloured picture postcard is of the Singapore Government House.

[21]
BEACH ROAD, SINGAPORE. (C 1910)

Back: Divided
Series and/or No.: 104
Publisher: Kong Hing Chiong & Co., North Bridge Road, Singapore

A picture postcard showing Beach Road, with the Hippodrome and Alhambra theatres on the right hand side.

[22]
SINGAPORE, CHINATOWN, II. (C 1905)

Cancellation: Nil (only for use in Hong Kong)
Back: Undivided
Series and/or No.: 120

This postcard depicts a street scene in Singapore Chinatown with a rickshaw puller and a bullock-cart.

The Esplanade, Singapore.

[23]
THE ESPLANADE, SINGAPORE. (C 1940)

Cancellation: 1941
Back: Divided

The Esplanade, Singapore, a black and white real photographic card sent from Singapore to USA.

[24]

Untitled [A road scene in Singapore].
(c 1897)

Cancellation: 1901
Back: Undivided
Publisher: Not stated. Attributed to G.R. Lambert & Co., Singapore

A road (possibly Orchard Road) at the end of the 19th century with a rickshaw in the foreground and two men with umbrellas by its side. The road is well shaded with tall trees, and there are houses in the background.

[25]

Untitled [A young Malay man].

Cancellation: 1901
Back: Undivided
Publisher: Not stated. Attributed to G.R. Lambert & Co., Singapore

This postal stationery picture postcard shows a young Malay man (possibly a prince) occupying its left hand side.

[26]
Untitled [Collyer Quay]. (c 1890)

Cancellation: 1901
Back: Undivided
Publisher: Not stated. Attributed to G.R. Lambert & Co., Singapore

Collyer Quay and the waterside with rickshaws and hackney carriages along rows of offices. There are many sampans in the foreground.

[27]
Untitled [Collyer Quay]. (c 1890)

Cancellation: 1901
Back: Undivided
Publisher: Not stated. Attributed to G.R. Lambert & Co., Singapore

The scene is that of Collyer Quay [26], but with a closer-up view and less animation.

[28]

Untitled [A Chinese festival]. (c 1890)

Back: Undivided
Publisher: Thomas De La Rue Co., London

A festival (likely to be a Chingay procession during the Chinese New Year) where young maidens were dressed up in their Peranakan fineries and paraded on horses and carriages drawn by bullocks. This is a rare unused postal stationery picture postcard.

[29]

SCHWEIZER SCHUTZEN VEREIN. SINGAPORE. [Shooting Range, Swiss Shooting Club, Singapore.] (C 1895)

Cancellation: 1902
Back: Undivided
Publisher: Not stated. Attributed to G.R. Lambert & Co., Singapore

The Swiss Shooting Club was started in 1871 in Balestier. After the First World War, the Club was renamed the Swiss Club.

[30]
CLUB HAUS, SCHWEIZER SCHUTZEN VEREIN. SINGAPORE.
[Club House, Swiss Shooting Club, Singapore.]

Cancellation: 1902
Back: Undivided
Publisher: Not stated. Attributed to G.R. Lambert & Co., Singapore

A front view of the Swiss Shooting Club's Club House in Singapore.

[31]
CLUB HAUS, SCHWEIZER SCHUTZEN VEREIN. SINGAPORE.
[Club House, Swiss Shooting Club, Singapore.]

Cancellation: 1902
Back: Undivided
Publisher: Not stated. Attributed to G.R. Lambert & Co., Singapore

The view of the Club House closely resembles [30] but was taken from the back. A flag-pole on the left can also be seen.

[32]

Untitled [A Chinese Barber with his customer].

Cancellation: 1901
Back: Undivided
Publisher: G.R. Lambert & Co., Singapore

An itinerant Chinese barber digging the ear of a
customer on the side of the road.

[33]

Chinese Girl. (c 1900)

Cancellation: 1901
Back: Undivided
Series and/or No.: 22
Publisher: Max H. Hilckes, Singapore

This postcard depicts a young Peranakan girl dressed
as a bridesmaid standing besides a draped chair.

[34]
KLING BOY.

Cancellation: 1901
Back: Undivided
Series and/or No.: 324
Publisher: G.R. Lambert & Co., Singapore

An Indian boy sitting on a rock.

[35]
Untitled [A young Indian man].

Cancellation: 1902
Back: Undivided
Publisher: G.R. Lambert & Co., Singapore

In this postcard, a young Indian man is dressed in a striped shirt, is bare-footed and carrying a walking stick.

[36]
Untitled [A Chinese rattan repairer].

Cancellation: 1901
Back: Undivided
Publisher: G.R. Lambert & Co., Singapore

This postcard depicts a Chinese rattan repairer
with a straw hat.

[37]
Untitled [Rickshaw pullers].

Cancellation: 1901
Back: Undivided
Publisher: Not stated. Attributed to G.R. Lambert &
Co., Singapore

A black and white photograph of rickshaw pullers
stopping to eat hawkers' food under a shady tree.

[38]

SNAKE CONJURER.

Cancellation: 1901
Back: Undivided
Series and/or No.: 354
Publisher: Not stated. Attributed to G.R. Lambert
& Co., Singapore

Depicting a bearded Sikh snake charmer with his
flute and two cobra snakes on a table.

[39]

Untitled [Traditionally dressed Malay women]. (c 1895)

Cancellation: 1901
Back: Undivided
Publisher: Not stated. Attributed to G.R. Lambert & Co.,
Singapore

Two young Malay women dressed in *baju panjang* with
sarong and wearing jewelleries, sitting on a couch in the
studio of G.R. Lambert.

[40]

COUNTRY ROAD.

Cancellation: 1901
Back: Undivided
Publisher: G.R. Lambert & Co., Singapore

A rural scene of tall trees and two European men with hats standing at a gate.

[41]

SINGAPORE, WITH BEST COMPLIMENTS! (c 1897)

Cancellation: 1897
Back: Undivided
Publisher: Not stated. Attributed to G.R. Lambert & Co., Singapore

This is a black and white ink-sketched drawing of a sailing boat by the Singapore shoreline, with the Dalhousie Obelisk and St. Andrew's Cathedral in the background.

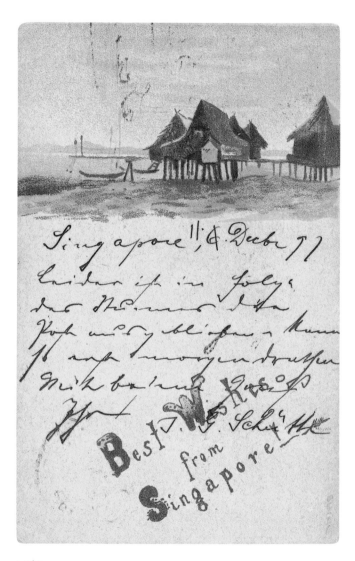

[42]
GREETING FROM SINGAPORE. (1897)

Cancellation: 1897
Back: Undivided
Publisher: Not stated. Attributed to G.R. Lambert & Co., Singapore

A black and white ink-sketched drawing depicting a star-filled night in Singapore, and featuring a large crescent moon. It was lightly painted in blue to give it a nightglow effect. This scene in the postcard is the most common of the postal stationery picture postcards.

[43]
BEST WISHES FROM SINGAPORE.

Cancellation: 1897
Back: Undivided

This postcard depicts Malay fishing huts by the seashore.

[44]
SINGAPORE. GREETING FROM. (1897)

Cancellation: 1897
Back: Undivided
Publisher: Not stated. Attributed to G.R. Lambert
& Co., Singapore

A picturesque scene of the Hotel de l'Europe
amidst bright orange flame-of-the-forest trees.

[45]
GREETING FROM SINGAPORE.

Cancellation: 1897
Back: Undivided
Publisher: Not stated. Attributed to G.R. Lambert
& Co., Singapore

Two huts and a coconut tree within a circular
frame are printed on this postcard.

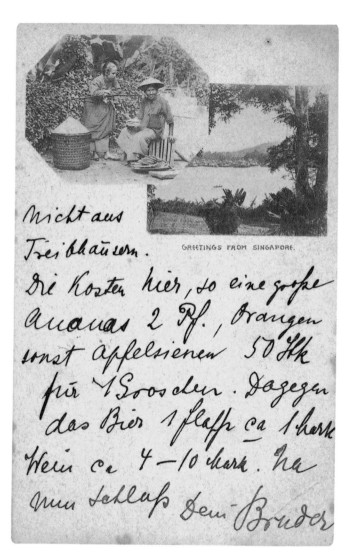

GREETINGS FROM SINGAPORE.

GREETINGS FROM SINGAPORE.

[46]
GREETINGS FROM SINGAPORE. (C 1890)

Back: Undivided
Publisher: Not stated. Attributed to G.R. Lambert
& Co., Singapore

A typical busy scene of the Cavenagh Bridge
with many horse carriages. The postcard was
colour-tinted manually.

[47]
GREETINGS FROM SINGAPORE.

Back: Undivided
Publisher: Not stated. Attributed to G.R. Lambert & Co., Singapore

This postcard has two views: (left hand side) a Malay woman
patronising a Malay hawker; (right hand side) a rectangular view of
St. James looking across to Pulau Brani (c 1895). St. James was a
promontory lying between the Blangah Bay and Sibet Bay.

[48]

GREETINGS FROM SINGAPORE. (C 1890)

Back: Undivided
Publisher: Not stated. Attributed to G.R. Lambert
& Co., Singapore

This postcard closely resembles [46], but the
colours are much less pronounced.

[49]

GREETINGS FROM SINGAPORE.

Cancellation: 1898
Back: Undivided
Publisher: Not stated. Attributed to G.R. Lambert
& Co., Singapore

There are two views in this postcard: (left hand
side) a Malay boy sits on a bench; (right hand
side) the view from Johnston's Pier (c 1890).

The SINGAPORE RIVER and WATERFRONT

Anderson Bridge, the first bridge across the mouth of the Singapore River, shown here soon after its opening in 1910.
(*See* [54])

A scene of North Boat Quay around 1930, with the Read Bridge in the background.
(*See* [57])

The Singapore River

Sir Stamford Raffles founded Singapore in 1819 as a commercial outpost of the British East India Company to counter Dutch supremacy in Southeast Asia, and to further the company's trade with China. After securing British interest in the island by a signed agreement with the Temenggong on 6 February 1819, Sir Stamford Raffles wrote: "This place possesses an excellent harbour and everything that can be desired for a British port... we have commanded an intercourse with all the ships passing through the Straits of Singapore. In short, Singapore is everything we could desire, and I may consider myself most fortunate in the selection; it will soon rise into importance..."[25]

"The Singapore River once played a vital role in our history... it was an economic and trading artery of colonial Singapore. From the warehouses and trading offices along the river stretched a trading network which encompassed much of island Southeast Asia. The Singapore River was also a mart where the diverse migrant communities, which made up colonial Singapore, worked out how best to live harmoniously with their fellow men and trading rivals... the early pioneers have passed on..."[25]

The Singapore River has since passed on from being a river of transport and commerce[25] to a river of cruises and pleasure.[26] When the first ppcs of Singapore were issued in 1897, the Singapore River was already well developed as the economic and trading artery of Singapore. By the time our survey of ppcs of Singapore ends with the Japanese Occupation (1942–1945), the economic importance of the Singapore River had declined.

The best view of a river is from an aerial view; we begin our survey of the Singapore River with its aerial panoramic views [50; 51]. As one sails upwards from the river's mouth [52; 53], the position of the river is marked by five bridges. The first bridge is Anderson Bridge [54 (*left, top*)]; it was named after Sir John Anderson (Governor, Straits Settlements, 1904–1911); it was opened on 12 March 1910. The second bridge is Cavenagh Bridge [55]; it was built in 1869; initially named Edinburgh Bridge, the name was later changed to honour Colonel Orfeur Cavenagh (Governor, Straits Settlements, 1859–1867). Cavenagh Bridge is the most photographed bridge; one of Singapore's early postal stationery ppc (c 1897) [46] features this bridge. Singapore's third bridge, Elgin Bridge [56] is actually its earliest; it was built in 1823 and linked South and North Bridge Roads. Originally a wooden bridge named Thomson Bridge, it was replaced in 1862 by an iron bridge called Elgin Bridge after Lord Elgin (Governor-General of India, 1862–1863). A new Elgin Bridge (higher and wider with arched railings) was constructed in 1927. Moving up the river, the fourth bridge is Coleman Bridge; this bridge is seldom photographed. Further upstream, the fifth bridge is Read Bridge [57 (*left, middle*)]; named after William Read, a prominent merchant who successfully petitioned for the S.S. to be ruled directly from London as a Crown Colony. It was built in 1889 to replace Merchant Bridge (it was too low for tongkangs (barges) to pass under). It was also known as Melaka Bridge due to its proximity to Kampong Melaka.

Sir Stamford Raffles allotted the best part of the river (the area near its mouth) to the Europeans; thus John

Cameron in 1856 wrote: "From the river's entrance to this Bridge (Elgin Bridge), on town side, a long range of godowns extend, forming a complete crescent. The nearer the entrance are occupied by Europeans, but all the godowns further up are the property of Chinese… On the eastern bank of the river for a considerable way up there are no houses, the land having been reserved for Government purposes."[25]

Collyer Quay, Old Harbour and Waterfront

Collyer Quay was featured in the first postal stationery picture postcards produced by G.R. Lambert in 1897 [26; 27]. Collyer Quay was named after George Collyer, the Madras Engineer who designed an extensive reclamation scheme for the seafront; it was completed in 1864. By 1866, the ensemble of new buildings, constructed as uniform as possible along the Quay, was completed much to the great delight of the business community. The buildings were soon acknowledged as "one of the sights of the Far East".[27] This explains why Collyer Quay appears so frequently in early Singapore ppcs.

Four early views of Collyer Quay between 1898 to 1902 are shown in [60-63]. Johnston's Pier, along Collyer Quay, was named after Alexander Johnston; a doyen of the European mercantile community and who in 1820, founded the firm of A.L. Johnston & Co. Johnston's Pier was built in 1855 and until its demolition in 1933, it was the main city landing point [61; 63]. Johnston's Pier was replaced by Clifford Pier [67]. Besides the Hong Kong and Shanghai Bank, other handsome buildings lined Collyer Quay [64; 65 (*right, top*)]. The transformation of Collyer Quay is shown in [60-66].

It is a common fallacy that Clifford Pier was built on the site of Johnston's Pier; it was actually built much further along Collyer Quay (Ray Tyers, 1976)[9]. Clifford Pier was named after Sir Hugh Clifford (Governor, Straits Settlements, 1927–1929). "Names die hard and even today if you ask the taxi driver or the sampan operator

to take you to Johnston's Pier or Lampu Merah (Malay for red lamp) you would be taken to Clifford Pier. A red oil lamp used to hang on the end of Johnston's Pier as a warning to shipping in the roads."[9]

In the early 1900s, sailing ships arriving in Singapore would often be anchored along the roads while smaller vessels such as sampans would ferry passengers and goods to Collyer Quay [68; 69]. The waterfront that greeted visitors is shown in [70-73].

New Harbour, Keppel Harbour

During the 14th century, Chinese seafarers had discovered the Keppel Harbour channel; they called it "Dragon's Teeth Gate", naming it after the two rocky outposts that "guarded" the harbour's entrance. William Farquhar, the First Resident of Singapore, referred to it as the New Harbour in 1820; its name was changed to Keppel Harbour [74; 75 (*right, middle*)] in 1900.[4] The Straits of Singapore gained in importance as the main shipping channel. In 1823, the earliest port regulations promulgated Sir Stamford Raffles' declaration that "… the Port of Singapore is a Free Port and the trade there is open to ships and vessels of every nation free of duty, equally and alike to all…"[28] Development was rapid and this resulted in the Singapore River and the old harbour at Collyer Quay becoming congested; Keppel Harbour was opened for ocean-going vessels in 1852.[28] In 1866, Tanjong Pagar Dock Company was opened for business; in 1885, Borneo Wharf was opened. In 1912, the Singapore Harbour Board was constituted under the Straits Settlements Ports Ordinance.[4, 28]

Keppel Harbour was named after Admiral Sir Henry Keppel; he was admired by all who came in contact with him.[9] Two views of Tanjong Pagar Wharf are shown in [76]. Borneo Wharf[a] is shown in [78; 79]. Victoria Dock [80] was opened and named by Sir Harry Ord on 17 October 1868[29]. King's Dock [81], the second largest dock in the world then, was opened in 1911.[9]

Winchester Building along Collyer Quay in 1910, where the office of Great Eastern Life Assurance Co. Ltd was situated.
(*See* [65])

A view of the Keppel Harbour from the top of Mount Faber in 1910.
(*See* [75])

[50]
Untitled [Singapore River, Boat Quay].
(c 1930)

Cancellation: 1932
Back: Divided

An aerial view of the crescentic shape of Boat Quay crowded with twakows, tongkangs and sampans.

[51]
BOAT QUAY, SINGAPORE. (C 1930)

Cancellation: 1933
Back: Divided

A panoramic aerial shot of the congested Singapore River with rows of Chinese merchant shophouses and godowns along its bank.

[52]

MOUTH OF SINGAPORE RIVER. (C 1900)

Cancellation: 1906
Back: Undivided
Series and/or No.: 28702
Publisher: G.R. Lambert & Co., Singapore

Loaded tongkangs and twakows going upstream past the mouth of the Singapore River with their cargoes.

[53]

SINGAPORE RIVER & DRILL HALL. (C 1906)

Back: Divided
Publisher: Koh & Co., Singapore

The Drill Hall at the mouth of the Singapore River. It was built for the Singapore Volunteer Artillery in 1891; it was dismantled in 1907 and re-erected at Beach Road.

Anderson Bridge, Singapore

[54]
ANDERSON BRIDGE, SINGAPORE.

Back: Divided
Publisher: Japanese

Anderson Bridge, the first bridge across the mouth of the Singapore River, shown here soon after its opening in 1910.

Singapore.

[55]
Untitled [Cavenagh Bridge]. (1902)

Cancellation: 1902
Back: Undivided

This postcard is uncommon as it has a Queen Victoria S.S. postage stamp on the picture side.

Singapore. Boat Quay.

[56]

SINGAPORE. BOAT QUAY. (1907)

Cancellation: 1907
Back: Divided
Publisher: Wilson & Co., Orchard Road, Singapore

A bustling scene of Boat Quay, with the Coleman Bridge in the background.

North Boat Quay, Singapore.

[57]

NORTH BOAT QUAY, SINGAPORE. (C 1930)

Back: Divided
Series and or No.: 1025
Publisher: The Continental Stamp Company, Singapore

A scene of North Boat Quay, with the Read Bridge in the background.

Boat Quay and Bullocks, Singapore.   No. 5

[58]
BOAT QUAY AND BULLOCKS, SINGAPORE.
(C 1910)

Back: Divided

Bullock-carts were used to transport wood in the
early 1900s.

(29)   Landing of rice by Chinese coolies at Boat Quay, Singapore.

[59]
LANDING OF RICE BY CHINESE COOLIES AT
BOAT QUAY, SINGAPORE. (1916)

Cancellation: 1916
Back: Divided
Series and/or No.: 29

Depicting the economic prosperity and busy
activities of daily living at Boat Quay and along
the Singapore River.

Singapore. Johnston's Pier and Collyer Quay.

[60]
SINGAPORE. JOHNSTON'S PIER AND
COLLYER QUAY.

Cancellation: 1902
Back: Undivided

The postcard comes affixed with a S.S. Queen
Victoria 1¢ stamp; such postcards are rare.

Singapore. Johnstons Pier and Collyer Quay.

[61]
SINGAPORE. JOHNSTON'S PIER AND
COLLYER QUAY.

Cancellation: 1905
Back: Undivided

A view of Johnston's Pier before it was replaced
by Clifford Pier.

Collyer Quay and part of Hongkong Bank.

[62]
COLLYER QUAY AND PART OF HONG KONG BANK. (C 1900)

Cancellation: 1901
Back: Undivided

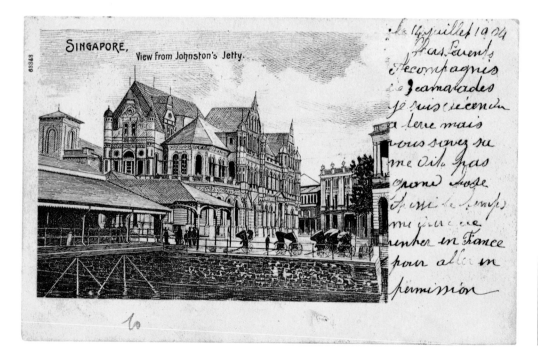

SINGAPORE, View from Johnston's Jetty.

[63]
SINGAPORE. VIEW FROM JOHNSTON'S PIER. (C 1900)

Cancellation: 1904
Back: Undivided
Series and/or No.: 63343

The ornate building opposite the pier is the Hong Kong and Shanghai Bank.

[64]

COLLYER QUAY, SINGAPORE. (C 1910)

Back: Divided

Showing the head office of the Hong Kong and Shanghai Bank Corporation built in 1892 on the site of the A.L. Johnston Company's building in Collyer Quay, opposite Johnston's Pier.

[65]

Untitled [Winchester Building]. (c 1910)

Back: Divided

Winchester Building along Collyer Quay where the office of Great Eastern Life Assurance Co. Ltd was situated.

[66]
JOHNSTON'S PIER. SINGAPORE. (C 1930)
Back: Divided

[67]
SINGAPORE. THE NEW PIER. (C 1933)
Back: Divided

Clifford Pier replaced Johnston's Pier after it was demolished in 1933.

The Roads with sampanes, Singapore.

[68]

THE ROADS WITH SAMPANS, SINGAPORE. (C 1900)

Back: Undivided

Publisher: Hartwig & Co. Succ., Singapore

Sampans ferrying goods on the way to Collyer Quay.

Singapore Roads.

[69]

SINGAPORE ROADS.

Cancellation: 1905

Back: Divided

Publisher: German

This colourful postcard shows sampans being guided alongside a steamer.

[70]
SINGAPORE BREAK WATER. (C 1930)

Back: Divided
Series and/or No.: 284

An American barge approaching the "Break Water" before reaching Collyer Quay.

[71]
GENERAL VIEWS – SINGAPORE. (C 1925)

Cancellation: 1932
Back: Divided

A photographic postcard showing the waterfront along Collyer Quay (top); a panorama which includes Empress Place and the Padang (below). The three domed buildings along Collyer Quay (starting from the left) are: the Second Ocean Building, the Maritime Building and the Hong Kong Bank Chamber.

[72]
Untitled [Sea view of Collyer Quay]. (c 1930)
Back: Divided

With a closer sea view of Collyer Quay, this postcard shows the Johnston's Pier with the Maritime Building, the Hong Kong Bank Chamber and Fullerton Building in the background.

[73]
VIEW TAKEN FROM SEA, SINGAPORE. (C 1940)
Back: Divided

This photographic postcard shows (from its right) the Clifford Pier with the Ocean Building and Alkaff Building.

[74]
SINGAPORE. ENTRANCE TO NEW-HARBOUR.
(C 1900)

Cancellation: 1906
Back: Undivided

Offering a bird's-eye view of the entrance to
Singapore's New Harbour.

[75]
SINGAPORE. KEPPEL HARBOUR. (1910)

Cancellation: 1910
Back: Divided
Publisher: Wilson & Co., Orchard Road, Singapore

A view of the Keppel Harbour from the top of
Mount Faber.

[76]
Untitled [Two views of Tanjong Pagar Wharf]. (1905)

Cancellation: 1905
Back: Undivided
Series and/or No.: 70857

Shot from two different angles, the pictures on the postcard afford one contrasting views of the Tanjong Pagar Wharf.

[77]
EMBARQUEMENT DU CHARBON A SINGAPOUR. [Loading coal onto a French steamer.] (c 1910)

Back: Divided
Publisher: Devambez, Grav, Editeur, France

This postcard has a serrated lower border; it was detached from a menu for first-class passengers on the steamer.

55

Singapore. Borneo Wharf (French Mailsteamer).

[78]
SINGAPORE. BORNEO WHARF (FRENCH MAILSTEAMER). (1907)

Cancellation: 1907
Back: Divided

This picture on the postcard captures a photograph of a French Mailsteamer unloading its cargo at the Singapore Borneo Wharf.

German Mail steamer at Borneo Wharf. SINGAPORE.

[79]
GERMAN MAIL STEAMER AT BORNEO WHARF. SINGAPORE. (1907)

Cancellation: 1907
Back: Divided
Publisher: G.R. Lambert & Co., Singapore

Coolies are loading the ship with its cargo; Europeans donning white jackets and hats are boarding the steamer.

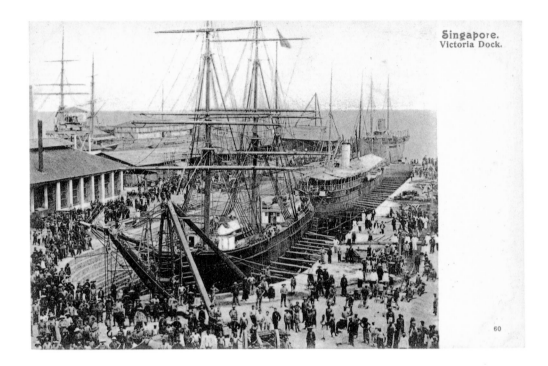

[80]
SINGAPORE. VICTORIA DOCK. (c 1910)

Back: Divided

A large crowd at what could be the Victoria Dock's opening ceremony.

[81]
Untitled [The Biggest Dock in the East called the King's Dock in Singapore]. (c 1913)

Back: Divided

A rare photographic postcard showing two views of the King's Dock.

EMPRESS PLACE and COMMERCIAL HUB

The Victoria Theatre and Memorial Hall around 1910.
(*See* [82])

Looking towards the tower of the Victoria Memorial Hall (c 1906); the General Post Office and Exchange Building is on the right.
(*See* [94])

Empress Place (Queen's Place)

Near the mouth of the Singapore River is Empress Place; it was named in 1907 after Queen Victoria.[30,31] Empress Place is dominated by the Victoria Theatre and Memorial Hall, the Government Secretary Office and the Dalhouise Obelisk [82 (*left, top*); 83]. The Victoria Theatre and Memorial Hall was first built as a town hall in 1862. In 1905, the Victoria Memorial Hall was built [84]. Next to the Town Hall, a central clock tower was added in 1906. In 1980, the Memorial Hall was extensively renovated and renamed the Victoria Concert Hall.[9]

The Dalhouise Obelisk [83-86] was erected to commemorate the visit of the Marquis of Dalhouise, Governor-General of India, to Singapore in 1850. It was designed by J.T. Thompson (Government Architect and Surveyor, 1841–1853). Originally sited at the river end of High Street, opposite the Dalhouise Pier (Harbour Pier), it was shifted in 1890 (due to land reclamation to enlarge the Padang) nearer to the Victoria Memorial Hall and finally in 1911 to its present site further from the Hall.[9]

The bronze elephant [86; 87] in front of Victoria Memorial Hall was a gift to Singapore from King Chulalongkong (Rama V) of Siam (Thailand) as a token of gratitude for the hospitality he received when he visited Singapore in 1871. It was shifted to the front of Parliament House in 1919 to make way for the statue of Sir Stamford Raffles.[9]

The bronze statue of Sir Stamford Raffles [88; 89] was unveiled on the Padang in 1887, the same year as Queen Victoria's golden jubilee. It was moved to its present position in front of the Victoria Memorial Hall in 1919 as part of Singapore's Centenary Celebrations; the tablet beneath the statue was unveiled [88] by Sir Arthur Young (Governor, Straits Settlements, 1911–1920). The Empress Place Building (adjacent to the River): the central part of this conglomerate of buildings [90; 91] is the oldest and was built in 1864–1865 as the new Court House. New wings were added in the later years and the offices housed within included the Secretariat and the Audit Department among others.[32]

Fullerton Square and Battery Road

Fullerton Square and Building [96-99] were named after Robert Fullerton, the first Governor of the Straits Settlements. Fullerton Square (c 1900–1910) is shown in [94 (*left, middle*); 95] depicting the General Post Office, Exchange Building and Flint's Building. The Singapore Club is shown in [92] with the Tan Kim Seng Fountain. The Tan Kim Seng Fountain was installed in Fullerton Square in 1882[32] in honour of Tan Kim Seng (1805–1864) who donated $13,000 in 1857 to bring a better supply of water into town.[33] Another landmark building in Fullerton Square is the departmental store, Whiteaway Laidlaw & Co. [93]. It was established in Singapore in 1900 and its building in Fullerton Square was built in 1910 to replace Flint Building.[29]

Battery Road [100-104] connects Fullerton Square to Raffles Place; it was so named for it used to lead to Fort Fullerton. The Chinese Hokkiens referred to it as *tho kho an* (at the back of the godowns), an allusion to the number of European and Chinese godowns that were located along the road.[32]

The Medical Hall Ltd [101; 102] (23 Battery Road) stood prominently at the Fullerton Square end of Battery

Road. "One of the most flourishing business of its kind is the Medical Hall, founded as far back as 1882 as a firm of dispensing chemists, at the well known corner opposite the General Post Office."[18]

The well known publisher of picture postcards, C.A. Ribeiro & Co. Ltd was located in Battery Road [100]. Banks such as the Bank of Taiwan and the Chartered Bank [103 (*right, top*)] were also located in Battery Road. Flint Street [105] was named after Captain William Flint (1781–1828), brother-in-law of Sir Stamford Raffles.[32]

Raffles Place and Vicinity

Raffles Place was also known as Commercial Square. It was developed in 1823–1824 on direct order from Sir Stamford Raffles. Originally a swamp before it was laid with flowers and trees (the Chinese Hokkien name for it was *hua hooi kak* (flower garden corner)[32], Commercial Square was officially renamed Raffles Place in 1858.

Raffles Place before 1850 [106] was an open space with gardens in its midst; the landmark in the foreground was the Gemmill Fountain. The fountain was presented by John Gemmill in 1864; he was Singapore's first auctioneer.[29] Up till 1901, the roads around Raffles Place were red lateritic roads [107].

John Little & Co. Ltd [108 (*right, middle*); 109] dominated the eastern side of Raffles Place; it was established by Martin Little in 1842. Robinson & Co. [110; 111] was the other departmental store that stood out prominently at Raffles Place. It was founded in 1858 by Philip Robinson and James Gaborian Spicer.

The Arcade (Rubber share broker's den) [112] at the southeast of Raffles Place had a handsome Moorish façade. The Rubber Exchange Buildings were located at Robinson Road, adjacent to Raffles Place[35] [113]. The northwest corner of Raffles Place at the junction of Kling Street (now known as Chulia Street) and Bonham Street was dominated by the ornate Bonham Building which ran the full length of Bonham Street to Boat

Quay[4] [114; 115]. Bonham Street was named in 1858 after Sir Samuel George Bonham (Governor, Straits Settlements, 1837–1843)[32]. Chulia Street was so named because of the concentration of Indians from South India at the street.[32]

Robinson Road [117] was named after Sir William Robinson (Governor, Straits Settlements, 1877–1879). It was built on reclaimed land after the 1879 Telok Ayer Reclamation project. Market Street [116] ran between Cecil Street, the junction of Robinson Road and Cross Street; it was one of the early streets in colonial Singapore. It is also known in Hokkien as *tiong koi* meaning "Central Street".[32] Today, all the rows of handsome shophouses in Market Street have been demolished and it has become a small street sandwiched between the towering Republic Plaza and the Goldenshoe Car Park.

Finlayson Green [118], adjacent to Raffles Place was named after J. Finlayson, head of Boustead & Co. and Chairman of the Singapore Chamber of Commerce. The Straits Times, Borneo Co., Behn Meyer and other insurance and shipping companies were located here. The Netherland Hondete Bank [119] at the junction of Cecil and D'Almeida Streets, a stone's throw from Raffles Place, was also known as *Bank Blanda* (Malay for Dutch Bank). However, it started out as the Netherlands Trading Society way back in 1824.[36] At the end of Robinson Road is Anson Road; it was named after Sir Archibald Anson (Acting Governor, Straits Settlements, 1877). At the junction of Anson Road and Tanjong Pagar Road stood the Boustead Institute [120]. This Institute was named after Edward Boustead of Messers Boustead & Co.; on his death in 1891, he bequeathed £9,000 for the establishment of an institute for seamen. The Boustead Institute was opened on 2 July 1892 by Sir Cecil Clementi Smith (Governor, Straits Settlements, 1887–1893). There was also a "Singapore Sailors Institute" [121], situated in the vicinity of Anson and Robinson Roads.[37]

The Chartered Bank Building at the corner of Battery Road and Flint Street in 1910. (*See* [103])

The original John Little & Co. Ltd at Raffles Place, around 1900. (*See* [108])

[82]

SINGAPORE. VICTORIA THEATRE & MEMORIAL HALL. (C 1910)

Back: Divided
Series and/or No.: "Oilette" Series Postcard No. 8942
Publisher: Raphael Tuck & Sons, London

The Singapore Victoria Theatre and Memorial Hall without the Dalhouise Obelisk.

[83]

MEMORIAL HALL & GOVERNMENT SECRETARY OFFICE, SINGAPORE. (C 1915)

Back: Divided
Publisher: Russian

The Memorial Hall and Government Secretary Office with the Dalhouise Obelisk.

Queen Victoria Memorial Hall Singapore
in course of construction.

The Obelisk, Singapore.

[84]
QUEEN VICTORIA MEMORIAL HALL SINGAPORE
IN COURSE OF CONSTRUCTION. (1905)

Cancellation: 1907
Back: Divided
Publisher: Hartwig & Co., Succ, Singapore

This picture postcard was sent by Lee Kim San,
a well-known postcard collector, in 1910.

[85]
THE OBELISK, SINGAPORE. (1907)

Cancellation: 1907
Back: Divided

The Dalhouise Obelisk at the Padang
around the early 1900s.

Memorial Hall & Obelisk.

[86]
MEMORIAL HALL & OBELISK. (1911)

Cancellation: 1911
Back: Divided
Publisher: John Little & Co. Ltd, Singapore

A front view of the Bronze Elephant and Mortar in front of the Memorial Hall, including a side-view that overlooks the Singapore Cricket Club.

Monument of the Elephant presented by the King of Siam, Singapore.

[87]
MONUMENT OF THE ELEPHANT PRESENTED BY THE KING OF SIAM, SINGAPORE. (1916)

Cancellation: 1916
Back: Divided
Publisher: Russian

The bronze elephant was a gift to Singapore by King Chulalongkong of Siam as a token of gratitude for the hospitality he received during his visit in 1871.

[88]
VICTORIA MEMORIAL HALL. SINGAPORE.
(1919)

Back: Divided

This postcard shows the crowds outside the Victoria Theatre and Memorial Hall during the unveiling of the statue of Sir Stamford Raffles.

[89]
QUEEN'S PLACE SINGAPORE. (1926)

Back: Divided

The statue of Sir Stamford Raffles in front of Victoria Memorial Hall looking towards the Dalhousie Obelisk and Fullerton Building (which was under construction).

Government Secretary Office, Singapore.

[90]
GOVERNMENT SECRETARY OFFICE, SINGAPORE.
(1911)

Cancellation: 1911
Back: Divided
Series and/or No.: 37
Publisher: Russian

Some of the government offices located within
were the Secretariat, Audit Department and the
Education Department.

Government Buildings, Singapore.

[91]
GOVERNMENT BUILDINGS, SINGAPORE. (C 1900)
Back: Divided

The Supreme Court Building, looking towards
Victoria Memorial Hall.

[92]
SINGAPORE. THE SINGAPORE CLUB. (C 1910)

Back: Divided
Series and/or No.: "Oilette" Series
Publisher: Raphael Tuck & Sons, London

Despite the caption on the card, the building featured in the postcard is the Exchange Building, of which The Singapore Club was one of its tenants. The Tan Kim Seng Fountain is shown in the foreground.

63 •••

[93]
CAVANAGH BRIDGE SINGAPORE. (C 1910)

Back: Divided

This black and white photographic postcard gives the view of Whiteaway Laidlaw & Co. from Fullerton Square.

Cavanagh Bridge and General Post Office, Singapore.   No. 3

[94]
CAVANAGH BRIDGE AND GENERAL POST
OFFICE. SINGAPORE. (C 1906)

Back: Divided
Series and/or No.: 3

Looking towards the tower of the Victoria
Memorial Hall; the General Post Office and
Exchange Building is on the right.

Singapore. Post-Office and Exchange Building.

[95]
SINGAPORE. POST-OFFICE AND EXCHANGE
BUILDING. (1903)

Back: Undivided

Flint's Building (on the left hand side) housed
Emmerson's Tiffin rooms (the haunt of authors
like Joseph Conrad)[9].

[96]
Untitled [The Fullerton Building in construction]. (c 1926)

Back: Divided

A view of Anderson Bridge and the Fullerton Building under construction.

[97]
NEW BUILDING GENERAL POST OFFICE, SINGAPORE. (C 1926)

Back: Divided
Series and or No.: 1082
Publisher: The Continental Stamp Company, Singapore

A look at the Fullerton Building under construction. The building was to house the new General Post Office.

GENERAL POST OFFICE, SINGAPORE

[98]
GENERAL POST OFFICE, SINGAPORE. (C 1935)

Back: Divided

A view of the completed Fullerton Building (General Post Office) from the Singapore River. This postcard possesses a serrated edge as it has been torn out from a picture postcard booklet.

[99]
Untitled [Fullerton Building (General Post Office)]. (1940)

Cancellation: 1940
Back: Divided

The view of the Anderson Bridge and the Fullerton Building (General Post Office) from the Cricket Club.

Singapore,

Battery Road.

[100]
BATTERY ROAD. (C 1900)

Back: Undivided

The firm of C.A. Ribeiro & Co. was located on the ground floor shop (besides the lamp-post in the foreground).

Singapore. Battery Road.

[101]
SINGAPORE. BATTERY ROAD. (1902)

Cancellation: 1902
Back: Undivided

Battery Road looking towards Raffles Place with the Medical Hall on one side and the Chartered Bank on its opposite side.

[102]
BATTERY ROAD, SINGAPORE. (C 1906)

Back: Divided
Series and/or No.: 1042
Publisher: The Continental Stamp Company,
Singapore

Another postcard with the view of Battery Road
overlooking Raffles Place, with the Tan Kim Seng
Fountain in the foreground and the Hong Kong
and Shanghai Bank and the Memorial Hall
behind it.

[103]
BATTERY ROAD, SINGAPORE. (1910)

Cancellation: 1910
Back: Divided
Publisher: German

The Chartered Bank Building at the corner of
Battery Road and Flint Street.

[104]
SINGAPORE. BATTERY ROAD. (1912)

Cancellation: 1912
Back: Divided

Battery Road, as viewed from Raffles Place
looking towards Fullerton Square.

[105]
SINGAPORE. FLINT STREET. (C 1910)

Back: Divided
Series and/or No.: 3010
Publisher: Max H. Hilckes, Singapore

One can observe that the signboards visible on
top of the two-storey buildings include "The
Straits Advertising Co." and "The Insular Life
Assurance Co.".

[106]
RAFFLES SQUARE. (C 1890)

Cancellation: 1904
Back: Undivided
Series and/or No.: 78086

Raffles Square, with the Gemmill Fountain in the foreground; in the centre of the square stood large flame-of-the-forest trees.

[107]
RAFFLES PLACE, SINGAPORE. (C 1910)

Back: Divided
Publisher: Japanese

This is a view of Raffles Place around 1910.

[108]
JOHN LITTLE AT RAFFLES PLACE, SINGAPORE.
(C 1900)

Back: Divided

Notice the rickshaws on the red lateritic road.

Singapore. Raffle's Square.

[109]
SINGAPORE. RAFFLE'S SQUARE. (1904).

Cancellation: 1904
Back: Undivided

This postcard depicts John Little & Co. Ltd (left hand side) at Raffles Square. The postcard has been inaccurately spelt as Raffle's Square.

[110]
RAFFLES PLACE, SINGAPORE. (c 1910)

Back: Divided

Robinson & Co. housed in a building topped with the bronze statue of Mercury; note the many rickshaws outside it.

[111]
THE RAFFLES SQUARE SINGAPORE. (c 1926)

Cancellation: 1926
Back: Divided

A panoramic view of Raffles Square with John Little & Co. Ltd on the left and Robinson & Co. on the right. Note the heavy traffic of cars and rickshaws, as opposed to [107].

The Arcade (Rubber share brokers' den), Singapore.

Rubber Exchange Buildings, Singapore.

[112]
**THE ARCADE (RUBBER SHARE BROKERS' DEN),
SINGAPORE. (C 1910)**

Back: Divided
Publisher: Koh & Co., Singapore

The Arcade as situated at the southeast corner of
Raffles Place.

[113]
RUBBER EXCHANGE BUILDINGS, SINGAPORE. (C 1910)

Back: Divided
Publisher: Koh & Co., Singapore

The Rubber Exchange Buildings at Robinson Road,
adjacent to Raffles Place.

[114]
SINGAPORE RAFFLES PLACE/COMPLIMENTS OF
THE SEASON. (C 1900)

Cancellation: 1903
Back: Undivided

Depicting the northwest corner of Raffles Place
between Chulia Street (Kling Street) and Bonham
Street dominated by the ornate Bonham Building.

[115]
KLING STREET, SINGAPORE. (C 1910)

Back: Divided
Publisher: Russian

Kling Street was later renamed Chulia Street.

Market Street, Singapore.

[116]
MARKET STREET, SINGAPORE. (C 1910)

Back: Divided
Publisher: Kong Hing Chiong & Co., North Bridge Road, Singapore

This postcard shows Market Street running between Cecil Street and the junction of Robinson Road and Cross Street.

[117]
Untitled [Robinson Road and Market Street corner]. (1928)

Cancellation: 1928
Back: Divided

The triangular block in the centre is now the site of Tuan Sing Tower while the building on the right hand side has now been replaced by the Hong Leong Building.

(94)   Finlayson Green, Singapore.

Netherland Hondele Bank, Singapore.

[118]

FINALYSON GREEN, SINGAPORE. (1914)

Cancellation: 1914
Back: Divided
Publisher: Russian

Finalyson Green was named after J. Finalyson, Chairman of the Singapore Chamber of Commerce during that period of time.

[119]

NETHERLAND HONDELE BANK, SINGAPORE. (1922)

Cancellation: 1922
Back: Divided

Situated at the corner of Cecil and D'Almedia Streets, the Netherland Hondele Bank was the forerunner of "ABN AMRO" (a Dutch Bank).

[120]

SINGAPORE ANSON ROAD. (C 1900)

Back: Divided

Located at the junction of Anson Road and Tanjong Pagar Road; the Boustend Institute was for the use of seamen, seafaring men and dock employees.

[121]

SINGAPORE SAILORS INSTITUTE. (C 1930)

Back: Divided

Written but not posted, the message on the back of the postcard reads, "This is a fine place to spend a weekend"!

AROUND the PADANG

The statue of Sir Stamford Raffles on the Padang; facing the sea, in 1898. (*See* [122])

The Singapore Recreation Club facing the Padang in 1909. (*See* [130])

The Padang

The Padang (referred to in the past as the Plain, Cantonment Plain, Raffles Plain or the Esplanade) refers to the lush green field between the Singapore Cricket Club and the Singapore Recreation Club. In about 1890, the Esplanade was widened after land reclamation and another road called New Esplanade Road was built [124; 125]. In 1907, the area became known as the Padang and the roads around it were renamed – Esplanade Road became St. Andrew's Road and New Esplanade Road became Connaught Drive [127]; before reclamation, the seashore was where Connaught Drive is today.[32]

The Padang [126] became a major recreation area after the Singapore Cricket Club (1870) and the Singapore Recreation Club (1885) were built on either side of the field. After City Hall was built in 1929, the Padang became an Administrative Centre. The Padang is an intrinsic part of Singapore's history and heritage, and the stage for its pageant of memorable events.[32]

The 8 feet tall statue of Sir Stamford Raffles stood majestically in the centre of the Padang [122 (*left, top*); 123] facing the sea from 1887 to 1919. The statue was moved to the front of the Victoria Memorial Hall on 6 February 1919. The inscription on the pedestal reads, "This tablet to the memory of Sir Stamford Raffles to whose foresight and genius Singapore owes its existence and prosperity, was unveiled on 6 February 1919, the 100th anniversary of the foundation of the settlement."[31]

Between Connaught Drive and the sea is Elizabeth Park; on this park are the Cenotaph [132] and the Tan Kim Seng Fountain [133]. The Cenotaph is dedicated to the dead of the two world wars and was designed by Swan & MacLaren Architects. The foundation stone was laid on 15 November 1920 by Sir Laurence Guillemart (Governor, Straits Settlements, 1920–1927) and the Cenotaph was unveiled on 31 March 1922 by the Prince of Wales (later to be King Edward VIII and the Duke of Windsor). The beautiful Tan Kim Seng Fountain was originally erected in Fullerton Square in 1882 but was removed to Elizabeth Park in 1925 after the Fullerton Building was erected. The ornate fountain was built by Andrew Handyside & Co. Ltd, Derby and London.[9,31]

In the 1900s, four of Singapore's most famous hotels were to be found at and around the Padang: the Hotel de l'Europe (at the Padang); the Hotel de la Paix (at Coleman Street); the Adelphi Hotel (at Coleman Street) and the Raffles Hotel (at Beach Road, adjacent to the Padang). Of these, only the Raffles Hotel has flourished to this day.

The Singapore Cricket Club and the Singapore Recreation Club

The Singapore Cricket Club (SCC) was founded in 1859 and it has continued its existence till today. It is situated at the end of the Padang opposite the Victoria Memorial Hall. The third club house was built in 1877 [128] while the present club house was built in 1907, keeping the facade of the third building [129]. The SCC was active in cricket, rugby, tennis, lawn bowls, football and other outdoor sports as well as indoor games. Together with the Singapore Recreation Club (SRC), it maintains the Padang which till today is "the place to take in the air".[9] The SCC served the interest of the European community during the colonial days.

The SRC [130 (*left, middle*); 131] was founded in 1883; it occupies the other end of the Padang opposite St. Andrew's Cathedral. Its new building was opened on 2 September 1905. The SRC serves mainly the interest of the Eurasian community; its sporting activities include cricket, hockey and softball.[9]

Grand Hotel de l'Europe

The Grand Hotel de l'Europe was established in 1857 at the corner of High Street and Esplanade Road (St. Andrew's Road). The original structure of the hotel was modest [135] as compared to the "new" Hotel de l'Europe which opened in 1905 [136-139].

"It covers nearly an acre of ground and is of the Renaissance style of architecture. The ground floor façade consists of a series of segmented arches between massive rusticated piers, and forms a colonnade in front of the entrance hall, lounge, reading-room and bar along the Esplanade front; while the High Street side is divided into shops of good size… The building has been erected and furnished by Mr. N.N. Adis at a cost of a million dollars."[29] The Hotel de l'Europe was demolished in 1936.

The Supreme Court and City Hall

Following the closure and demolition of the Hotel de l'Europe in 1936; the Supreme Court was built on its site. The architect was F. Dorrington-Ward; the Corinthian columns, sculpture and facing were executed by the Italian artist Cavaliere Rodolfo Nolli. The Supreme Court was declared open by Sir Shenton Thomas (Governor, Straits Settlements, 1939–1942, 1945–1946). The Supreme Court is shown [134 (*right, top*)] soon after its opening.

City Hall was built in 1929 and its architect was F.D. Meadocrs. The site was adjacent to the Supreme Court on the site occupied by fine houses built by the famous architect G.D. Coleman; City Hall was originally called the Municipal Building [143].[9]

City Hall today provides the regular focal point for Singapore's important and festive occasions. As a building, City Hall is an enduring monument.

St. Andrew's Cathedral

On Coleman Street, adjacent to the Padang, stands St. Andrew's Cathedral [140-142; 144 (*right, middle*)]. The Cathedral stands nobly spired and white on a green sward beside the Esplanade. There was an earlier church on this site – St. Andrew's Church was built in 1835–1836 by Coleman. The tower and spire were later additions by J.T. Thomson. Twice the church was struck by lightning; the Cathedral was rebuilt by Indian convicts between 1856 and 1864.[30]

St. Andrew's Church/Cathedral was named after the Patron Saint of Scotland as the majority of the subscribers to the original building fund were Scots.[9]

The consecration of the Cathedral took place on 25 January 1862, on the Feast of Conversion of St. Paul.[9] The church once had a bell (the Revere Bell); the First American Consul in Singapore, Joseph Balestier, married Maria Revere in the Cathedral in 1843. Maria's father was a well known bell-maker in Boston, USA, and she presented the Revere Bell to the Cathedral in 1843. There it hung until it was removed to the National Museum in 1889.[30]

The Cathedral is rightly a place of memorials: the stained windows in the apse commemorates Sir Stamford Raffles, John Crawford and Major General W.J. Butterworth. The window at the Cathedral entrance was erected in memory of Colonel R. MacPherson, the designer and first builder of the Cathedral. MacPherson also has a granite monument with a Maltese Cross on top in the Cathedral grounds.[30]

Adelphi Hotel

The Adelphi Hotel [145-148] was at 1 and 2 Coleman Street (facing St. Andrew's Cathedral), and at the corner with North Bridge Road. It closed in 1973 and was demolished in 1980 to make way for the Adelphi Shopping Complex.

"One of the best known and most popular hotels in Singapore is the Adelphi Hotel. It was established in 1863 in Raffles Place, but the business soon outgrew the premises and a move was made to High Street, then to Coleman Street site… No better position than this could

The Supreme Court facing the Padang, soon after its opening in 1939.
(*See* [134])

The interior of the St. Andrew's Cathedral around 1930.
(*See* [144])

The Raffles Hotel around 1900.
(*See* [152])

The Raffles School (c 1910), a stone's throw away from the Padang.
(*See* [161])

have been selected, for the hotel is now within a short distance of all the principal places of business and Government Offices... Altogether the Adelphi is a most desirable place to stay at."[29]

Hotel de la Paix

The Hotel de la Paix [149-151] was located at 3 Coleman Street. It was also known as Burlington Hotel prior to Second World War; it was converted to shops and apartments after the war. It was demolished in the 1970s and on its site was built the Peninsular Hotel and Shopping Complex.[4,9] However, little else is known about this hotel, and in "One Hundred Years of Singapore" (1921),[29] there is no mention of the Hotel de la Paix, even though other nearby hotels such as the Raffles Hotel, Hotel de l'Europe and Adelphi Hotel are described in detail.

Raffles Hotel

The Raffles Hotel [152 (*left, top*); 153-159] is situated at 1–3 Beach Road, and it faces the Padang and the Esplanade. It was established in 1886 by the Armenian Sarkies brothers (Arshak, Aviet and Tigran); they undertook major renovations in 1889 to operate a building described as "a marvelous French Renaissance-style 'wedding cake'" by Ilsa Sharp.[30] The Bar and Billiard Room of the hotel in 1908 is shown in [155].

"The Raffles, as it developed, was instinct with Britishness. Somerset Maugham and Noel Coward were among its guests. British rubber planters from Malaya came down for a much needed change. The hotel catered to the rituals and victuals of colonial life, such as tiffin, tea dance and the cocktail hour... To former British civil servants and military men who choose to live out their lives in Singapore, the Raffles has a glory and a melancholy such as only the exiled heart can know."[30]

"It is a building of noble proportions and imposing appearance, and covers an area of no less than 200,000

square feet... On the ground floor is the marble-paved dining room... there is none more handsome in the East. The private dining rooms form an important feature, and are in constant demand for wedding breakfasts, private dinners... A large bar and smoke room is provided on the ground floor. There are over 150 suites of rooms. The cuisine is under the direct supervision of two accomplished European chefs..."[29]

The Raffles Hotel and Sea View Hotel were the only two hotels in Singapore to have a post office in their premises. The Raffles Hotel post office [158] functioned from about 1910 to 1929; in 1929 the post office was transferred to Raffles Institution.

The Raffles Hotel [159] has continued to flourish till today; even during the Japanese Occupation (1942 to 1945), it continued to function to serve the Japanese Military; it was then called Syonanto Hotel.

Raffles School/Institution

It was Raffles' dream to cater for formal education in Singapore. In 1823, he laid the foundation stone of an education institution "for the cultivation of Asian languages, the education of the sons of Malay rulers and the moral and intellectual improvement of the people of Asia".[5] The Raffles School is shown [161 (*left, middle*)] occupying a large area of land bounded by Stamford, North Bridge, Bras Basah and Beach Roads, a stone's throw away from the Padang. This building was largely credited to the work of G.D. Coleman who renovated the original building in 1835–1837. The three-storey block adjoining Bras Basah Road was built in 1875–1876. [161-163] depicts Raffles Institution around 1920. Not far from the Raffles School was the Waverley Hotel [160].

In 1967, the school relocated to Grange Road before moving to its present location in Bishan. The building was demolished in 1973 for the construction of Raffles City, a shopping mall today. Raffles Institution had a post office within its premise from 1929 to 1942.

ANDREWS CATHEDRAL & RAFFLES MONUMENT.

[122]
ANDREWS CATHEDRAL & RAFFLES MONUMENT.
(1898)

Back: Undivided
Publisher: Not stated. Attributed to Kunzli Freres, Zurich.

Showing the statue of Sir Stamford Raffles on the Padang; facing the sea.

Statue of Sir Stamford Raffles, Singapore.

[123]
STATUE OF SIR STAMFORD RAFFLES, SINGAPORE.
(C 1915)

Back: Divided
Publisher: Russian

The statue of Sir Stamford Raffles on the Padang; in the background is the Hotel de l'Europe.

Singapore. Esplanade.

The building in the centre, of the background is the pavillion, of the Singapore Cricket Club, JK

[124]
SINGAPORE. ESPLANADE. (C 1890)

Cancellation: 1904
Back: Undivided
Publisher: Not stated. Attributed to G.R. Lambert & Co., Singapore

Actually a photograph, it was later published as a postcard. The building is that of the Singapore Cricket Club.

The Esplanade, Singapore.

[125]
THE ESPLANADE, SINGAPORE. (C 1930)

Back: Divided
Series and/or No.: "Rapholette Glosso" Series
Publisher: Raphael Tuck & Sons, London

THE PADANG, SINGAPORE

COPYRIGHT PHOTOGRAPH
No. 8

[126]
THE PADANG, SINGAPORE. (C 1929)

Cancellation: 1929
Back: Divided
Publisher: Kelly & Walsh Ltd, Singapore

A photographic postcard of the Padang looking towards the Singapore Cricket Club.

CONNAUGHT DRIVE, SINGAPORE.

[127]
CONNAUGHT DRIVE, SINGAPORE. (C 1930)

Back: Divided

Connaught Drive with the Hotel de l'Europe to its right and the tower of the Victoria Memorial Hall in its centre.

Cricket Club.

[128]
CRICKET CLUB. (1903)

Cancellation: 1903
Back: Undivided

The Singapore Cricket Club's third building in 1903.

(25)   Singapore Cricket Club, Singapore.

[129]
SINGAPORE CRICKET CLUB. SINGAPORE. (C 1910)

Back: Divided

The new Singapore Cricket Club building, it was built in 1907 and it kept the centre portion of the third building.

Singapore Recreation Club, Singapore.

[130]
SINGAPORE RECREATION CLUB, SINGAPORE.
(1909)

Cancellation: 1909
Back: Divided

The Singapore Recreation Club facing the Padang.

Singapore Recreation Club, Singapore.

[131]
SINGAPORE RECREATION CLUB, SINGAPORE.
(1916)

Cancellation: 1916
Back: Divided
Publisher: Russian

A horse carriage is waiting outside the Singapore
Recreation Club.

[132]
Untitled [The Cenotaph]. (1935)

Cancellation: 1935
Back: Divided

The Cenotaph at Elizabeth Park; on the Cenotaph is chiselled "Our Glorious Dead".

Collyer Quay, Singapore.

[133]
Collyer Quay, Singapore. (1939)

Cancellation: 1939
Back: Divided

On the postcard is the Tan Kim Seng Fountain at Elizabeth Park; the Padang and Hotel de l'Europe are on its right hand side. The postcard has been inaccurately captioned as "Collyer Quay"; it is actually Elizabeth Walk.

The Supreme Court, Singapore.

[134]
THE SUPREME COURT, SINGAPORE.

Cancellation: 1939
Back: Divided

Offering the view of the Supreme Court facing
the Padang, soon after its opening in 1939.

Singapore.

[135]
Untitled [Hotel de l'Europe]. (c 1900)

Cancellation: 1905
Back: Undivided

This postcard was actually a photograph taken
around 1890, but it was later published as a
postcard around 1900.

[136]
Untitled [Hotel de l'Europe]. (c 1900)

Back: Undivided

This postcard affords one with a panoramic view of the Hotel de l'Europe with two Indian jugglers sitting outside.

[137]
THE EUROPE HOTEL LTD/SINGAPORE/THE SOCIAL CENTRE OF MALAYA. (C 1932)

Cancellation: 1932
Back: Divided

Depicting the interiors of the Hotel de l'Europe during the 1930s.

GRAND HOTEL DE L'EUROPE, SINGAPORE

[138]
GRAND HOTEL DE L'EUROPE, SINGAPORE.
(C 1910)

Publisher: Not stated. Attributed to Kunzli Freres, Zurich.

This postcard was actually used as a means to advertise the hotel.

Singapore. Hotel de l'Europe.

[139]
SINGAPORE. HOTEL DE L'EUROPE. (1918)

Back: Divided

The Hotel de l'Europe decorated for Armistice Day in 1918.

[140]

SINGAPORE – ST. ANDREW'S CATHEDRAL AND RAFFLES MONUMENT, ESPLANADE. (C 1909)

Cancellation: 1909
Back: Divided
Publisher: G.R. Lambert & Co. Ltd, Singapore

The statue of Sir Stamford Raffles standing "guard" in front of St. Andrew's Cathedral.

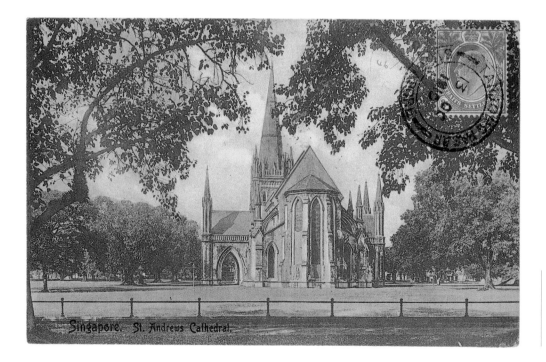

[141]

SINGAPORE. ST. ANDREW'S CATHEDRAL. (1910)

Cancellation: 1910
Back: Divided
Publisher: Wilson & Co., Orchard Road, Singapore

St. Andrew's Cathedral as pictured from its front during 1910.

[142]
ST. ANDREW'S CATHEDRAL, SINGAPORE. (1928)

Cancellation: 1928
Back: Divided

This postcard has a serrated left margin, which means it was torn from a postcard booklet.

[143]
MUNICIPAL BUILDING, SINGAPORE. (C 1934)

Cancellation: 1934
Back: Divided

The Municipal Building facing the Padang. Next to it is the Hotel de l'Europe; the spire of St. Andrew's Cathedral is behind it.

The Interior of St. Andrews Cathedral. *Singapore*

[144]
THE INTERIOR OF ST. ANDREW'S CATHEDRAL.
(C 1930)

Back: Divided
Publisher: G.R. Lambert & Co. Ltd, Singapore

92

Adelphi Hôtel — Singapore.

[145]
ADELPHI HOTEL – SINGAPORE. (C 1910)

Back: Divided
Series and/or No.: 12
Publisher: The Continental Stamp Company,
Singapore

[146]
LADIES LOUNGE, ADELPHI HOTEL, SINGAPORE.
(C 1905)

Back: Divided
Publisher: English

[147]
DINING HALL, SEALING 300 PERSONS/ADELPHI
HOTEL SINGAPORE. (C 1905)

Back: Undivided
Publisher: G.R. Lambert & Co. Ltd, Singapore

This spacious dining hall of the Adelphi Hotel
could easily accommodate up to 300 guests.

[148]
A Greeting from Singapore. (1901)

Cancellation: 1901
Back: Undivided
Publisher: Lithography of the Court i and 8.A.
Haase, Prague

A picture postcard with flowery borders depicting the Adelphi Hotel and its Billiard Room.

[149]
Singapore/Hotel de la Paix. (c 1900)

Cancellation: 1900
Back: Undivided

The hotel is shown together with a bullock-cart and an elephant. The postcard has foliate decorative margins.

[150]

SINGAPORE/HOTEL DE LA PAIX. (1901)

Cancellation: 1901
Back: Undivided
Publisher: Johs, Krogers, Buchdruckere I., Blan-Keneye, N., Hamburg, Germany

A postcard with views of Johnston's Pier and the sea-view looking towards the Padang

[151]

SINGAPORE/HOTEL DE LA PAIX. (C 1900)

A multiview postcard of the Johnston's Pier and the sea-view of the Esplanade looking into the Padang. This postcard's back was used to advertise a shop situated within the hotel.

[152]
THE RAFFLES HOTEL, SINGAPORE. (C 1900)

Cancellation: 1916
Back: Divided

This postcard was actually a photograph that was published as a postcard at a later date.

[153]
Untitled [The Raffles Hotel, Singapore].
(c 1902)

Cancellation: 1902
Back: Undivided

Featuring two views of the Raffles Hotel: its Main Building and its Dining Room.

[154]
Untitled [The Raffles Hotel, Singapore].
(c 1900)

Back: Divided
Publisher: G.H. Kiat & Co. Ltd, Singapore

Featuring the stylish façade and entrance of the
Raffles Hotel.

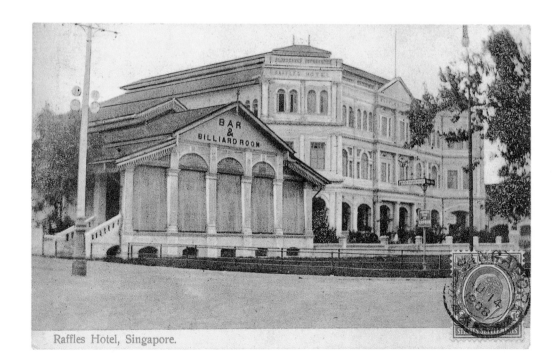

Raffles Hotel, Singapore.

[155]
RAFFLES HOTEL, SINGAPORE. (C 1908)

Cancellation: 1908
Back: Divided
Publisher: German

Depicting the Raffles Hotel's Bar and Billiard
Room.

RAFFLES HOTEL, SINGAPORE   Telegrams; "RAFFLES" SINGAPORE

THE FINEST BALLROOM IN THE EAST.

[156]
THE FINEST BALLROOM IN THE EAST. (C 1910)
Back: Divided
The Raffles Hotel's ballroom with several musicians on the stage.

SARKIES BROS. PROPRIETORS.

THE MAIN DINING HALL, RAFFLES HOTEL, SINGAPORE.

[157]
THE MAIN DINING HALL, RAFFLES HOTEL, SINGAPORE. (C 1910)
Back: Divided
Publisher: Photogravure, Waterlow & Sons Limited, London

[158]
Untitled [The Raffles Hotel, Singapore].
(1927)

Cancellation: 1927
Back: Divided

This postcard was posted from the Raffles Hotel's Post Office to Denmark. It is a scarce postmark on a postcard.

[159]
Untitled [Stylish doormen and porters of the Raffles Hotel]. (c 1920)

Back: Divided

Waverley-Hôtel.

[160]
WAVERLEY HOTEL. SINGAPORE. (C 1900)

Back: Undivided

The Waverly Hotel was situated along Hill Street and has since been demolished. However, little else is known about this hotel.

(19)   Raffles School, Singapore.

[161]
RAFFLES SCHOOL, SINGAPORE. (C 1910)

Back: Divided
Publisher: Russian

The Raffles School is shown occupying a large area of land bounded by Stamford, North Bridge, Bras Basah and Beach Roads, a stone's throw away from the Padang.

Raffles Institution, Singapore.

[162]
RAFFLES INSTITUTION, SINGAPORE. (C 1920)

Back: Divided

A sepia-toned photographic postcard of Raffles Institution during the 1920s.

Raffles Institution, Singapore.

[163]
RAFFLES INSTITUTION, SINGAPORE. (C 1920)

Back: Undivided
Publisher: German

CHINATOWN

The Thian Hock Keng Temple around 1930.
(See [166])

The Nagore Durgha around 1920.
(See [168])

Chinatown

"Close to the commercial heart of Singapore lies a nucleus of living spaces which has, even now, retained a special character. Games of Chinese chess still progress on five-foot-ways; medicinal herbs for every imaginable malady can be purchased; old men and women huddle in darkened alley-ways and congested cubicles; and shortly before the lunar new year the whole of Singapore seems to jostle together in one frenzied scramble to buy pussy willows, sweetmeats and other delicacies. All this and more is Chinatown."[38]

Sir Stamford Raffles' recommendations to the Town Committee were incorporated in the master plan drawn up by a Lieutenant Jackson in 1828: areas were specially allocated to the various racial groups. Chinatown had spread its roots on the southwest side of the Singapore River, where it has remained to this day.[32]

Physically, Chinatown may be loosely delineated as the area spanning Telok Ayer Street, South Bridge Road, New Bridge Road, Eu Tong Sen Street and its vicinity – the many small streets and lanes linking South Bridge Road with North Bridge Road. Telok Ayer Street was named after the Telok Ayer Bay [170], located at the foot of Mount Wallich. The Malay name refers to "bay water" because it was originally a coastal road along the bay. Telok Ayer Street [171] was the main commercial and residential thoroughfare in Singapore. In the past (before land reclamation), boats were moored at the bay, waiting to get water carried by bullock-carts from the well at Ann Siang Hill.[32]

The most photographed landmark on Telok Ayer Street is the Thian Hock Keng Temple [164-167; 166 (left, top)]. One of the best known temples in Singapore, it was built in 1839–1842. It is dedicated to the goddess Ma-Cho-Po or Tian Hou (Mother of Heavenly Sages);

other deities are Guan Di, Bao Sheng Da Di and Guan Yin.[39] Among its major financial backers were notable personalities such as Tan Tock Seng and Tan Kim Seng.[4, 39] In 1978, the temple was gazetted as a national monument because of its architectural quality and historical value.[39]

Another landmark at 140 Telok Ayer Street is the Nagoree Durgha (originally known as Shahul Durgha). It was built in 1828–1830 and is dedicated to the memory of the holy man, Sahul Hamid of Nagore. It is fascinating to observe how its combination of Palladian features on the street level contrasts perfectly with its Islamic balustrade above[30] [168 (left, middle); 169].

The first market in Singapore was located on the south bank of the Singapore River; it was moved to Telok Ayer in 1824. In the 1830s, there was a need for a bigger market and G.D. Coleman built a market in 1838 at Telok Ayer Bay; it was octagonal in shape. Due to land reclamation, a new market was built in 1894 on reclaimed land. Also octagonal in shape, it was meant to be a tribute to Coleman's market; the designer was James MacRitchie. The market at Robinson Road (Raffles Quay) was renovated and converted to a food centre in 1973. It is now colloquially known to the Chinese as Lau Pat Sat (Old Market), or to the Malays, Pasar Besi (Iron Market)[32] [172; 173].

The Wak Hai Cheng Bio on Philip Street [174] was built by the Teochews in 1850, and it functioned both as a temple and clan association. The building is still standing today.[5] The main deity in this temple is the Queen of Heaven; subsidiary deities are Long Wei Sheng Wang (The Sage King of the Dragon's Tail) and Tua Pek Kong. The roof is decorated with a colourful array of porcelain figurines of people, animals and pagodas. There is a large open courtyard in front of the temple[40].

The prewar image of Chinatown was that of narrow streets crowded with people, hawkers and jinrickshas [176-179] (*right, top*). Sago Lane was then infamous for its "death houses" (a sort of hospice where the terminally ill were brought to die). The Cantonese called Sago Lane "street of the dead". "Death houses" were eventually banned in 1961.[32] Near Sago Lane is Sago Street; in 1901 it had 14 brothels.[32, 38]

In the 1900s, the life of a jinricksha puller [180; 181] was hard and back-breaking; they also earned very little income. Many of the jinricksha pullers worked for a particular *kongsi* or *kun* (depot or station) which provided them lodging, the jinricksha and a small wage. Around 1900, many jinricksha depots were situated in Banda Street and other streets in Chinatown.[38]

Opium smoking was common among the Chinese in the 1900s[41] and was prevalent among the poor and the rich alike [182; 183]; rickshaw pullers smoked or (ingested) opium to keep them going in their hard jobs while the rich smoked opium for their addictive pleasures. Prominent doctors like Dr. Lim Boon Keng and Dr. Chen Su Lan[41] campaigned actively against the evils of opium smoking, but to no avail. Opium smoking continued in Singapore until the Japanese Occupation. Also, opium was a major source of revenue for the Colonial Government in the 1900s.[41]

Like the rickshaw pullers, many of the Chinese *ayahs* or *amahs* (servants) had their *kongsi* in Chinatown. These *amahs* were often Cantonese from Kwantung (China) and often wore white *samfoos* and black trousers [184 (*right, middle*); 185]. Many *samsui* (so called because many of them were from the Sam Sui district in China's Guangdong Province)[38] women also lived in Chinatown in Upper Chin Street (hence it was nicknamed "Black Cloth" Street).[38] These women were Hakka or Cantonese and wore red headgear and black/blue top and trousers.[38] They usually worked at construction sites or in road repairing [187].

The Chinese immigrants [186-193] frequented Chinese operas/wayangs [194; 195]. Smith Street used to have a theatrical hall (built in 1887) till 1940 when it started to show Chinese movies and its name was changed accordingly to Sun Seng Cinema.[38] Along Eu Tong Sen Street there were 2 theatrical halls: the Heng Seng Peng (Cantonese, Peiking and Hokkien operas) and the Heng Wai Sun (Cantonese operas).[38] [175; 197] show two hotels in Chinatown.

South Bridge Road

South Bridge Road [204; 207] is the road south of the Singapore River. It runs south of Elgin Bridge, hence its name. It is an extension of North Bridge Road and continues on to Maxwell Market. It is one of the major roads leading into Chinatown.[32] The Cantonese call it *ta ma lo* or "great horseway".[32]

In the 1900s, the four landmarks of South Bridge Road were the Central Police Station, the Police Court, the Sri Mariamman Temple and the Jamae Mosque. [196; 197]

The Jamae Mosque (218 South Bridge Road) [198] was built by the South Indian Muslims (known as *chulias*) who mostly comprised of traders and money-lenders. A *chulia* by the name of Amstar Saab built a mosque on South Bridge Road in 1826–1827 but it was replaced by the Jamae Mosque built between 1830 and 1835. A simple brick and plaster structure, it has a prayer hall with a spacious courtyard. It was gazetted as a national monument in 1974.[30]

The Sri Mariamman Temple (244 South Bridge Road) [199] was gazetted as a national monument in 1973. Naraina Pillay, the first Indian and Tamil pioneer of Singapore, built a temple of wood and atap in South Bridge Road in 1827; it was replaced by one of brick and plaster in 1843. Craftsmen from Madras were employed for their plaster skills. They incorporated models of Indian Sepoy soldiers into the crowd of figures on the

Sago Lane, Chinatown (c 1920), with many rickshaws by the roadside.
(*See* [176])

Chinese servants wearing *samfoos* and trousers, carrying their masters' babies.
(*See* [184])

The Jamae Mosque and the Sri Mariamman Temple in 1907.
(*See* [199])

The Chinese Protectorate of Singapore in 1907.
(*See* [216])

gopuram (tower gate) and walls of the temple. The Indian Sepoy soldiers images were erased in later renovations and now the sculptures are carved in Indian traditional costumes.[30]

The Central Police Station and the Police Court [200–202] were located along South Bridge Road; they were demolished in the 1970s. The Central Police Station (Headquarters) was Singapore's first central police station and was built in 1887, while the Police Court combined a Malay-style porch with a French mansard-style roof.[3,4] The Police Court was demolished in 1975 and is now the site of Hong Lim Shopping Centre.[3,4] Hong Lim Green was named after Cheang Hong Lim, an Opium and Spirit Farmer who was appointed a Justice of the Peace in 1873. Cheang was also responsible for converting the space in front of the Central Police Station into a public garden in 1876. Hong Lim Green was also used by the Straits Chinese Recreation Club as a recreation ground[33] [203]. The Straits Chinese Recreation Club was founded in 1884; its main purpose was to promote English outdoor sports such as lawn tennis, football, cricket, hockey and athletics. The name was later changed to the Singapore Chinese Recreation Club.[42]

Cross Street [205; 206] is one of the oldest streets of Singapore and it marks the western-most boundary of the first implementation of Sir Stamford Raffles' Plan of Chinatown.[32] It crosses South Bridge Road as it approaches Elgin Bridge. Many Chinese, Indians and Malays settled in Cross Street; the Chinese called it *kiat leng kia ko* (Kling man's street); the Indians called it *palkadei sadakku* (street of milk shops) while the Malays called it *kampong susu* (milk village).[32] Many Indian, Chinese and Malay shops and hawkers were found on Cross Street and the adjacent Hokien Street [208; 209]. Hokien Street is also one of the old streets of Singapore; many Hokkiens settled there: hence its name. The Chinese called it *cho be chai koi* (street where horse carriages are made).[32]

New Bridge Road

New Bridge Road [210–213] was built in 1842; Coleman Bridge links Hill Street with New Bridge Road. The Chinese call this road *sin pa sat ma chu cheng* (front of new market police station) or *ji ma lo* (number two horseway) or *gu chia chui* (Kreta Ayer). Many Teochew traders were located on New Bridge Road.[32]

Parallel to New Bridge Road is Eu Tong Sen Street; this street was named after the Penang-born millionaire tin miner, rubber estate and property owner, Eu Tong Sen (1877–1914). In 1919, he rebuilt the street and bought over the two existing Chinese opera theatres (Heng Seng Peng and Heng Wai Sun) [215]. Today on that plot of land was built the People's Park Complex.[32] Park Road [214] is adjacent to New Bridge Road.

Near New Bridge Road is Havelock Road; on it was sited the Chinese Protectorate from 1886 to 1930 [216 (*left, middle*)]. It was demolished in 1930 and in the space in front of it, a new building was built [217]; it is now known as the Ministry of Labour Building, and it was gazetted a national monument in 1998.[9,30] The first Chinese Protector was William Alexander Pickering (1886–1930), who brought about peaceful unity between the Chinese and other races in Singapore and Malaya. Two streets are named after him, one in Singapore and the other in Eastwood, England (his birth place).[9]

Neil Road

Neil Road is a continuation of South Bridge Road. The road was formerly known as Salat (Silat or Selat) Road. The Malay name was changed to Neil Road in 1858 to honour one of the British heroes in the 1857 Indian Mutiny, a Colonel Neil of the Madras Fusiliers. The Hokkiens call it *goo chia chwee sia lo* (steep street of Kreta Ayer).[32] Another interesting fact is that Lee Hoon Leong, grandfather of Minister Mentor (MM) Lee Kuan Yew, once lived at 147 Neil Road, with MM Lee living in that house for a few years.[32]

At the corner of Neil Road and Tanjong Pagar Roads stands the Jinricksha Station [218; 219]. It was built in 1880; the building still stands today; after the war it was a Family Planning Clinic; today it is a restaurant.

At the corner of Neil Road (89 Neil Road) and Craig Road is a handsome three-storey building with a large and striking octagonal cupola that was once known as the *Eng Aun Tong* or "The Tiger Medical Hall" [220; 221]. It was the Singapore Head Office cum factory of the Hakka Aw brothers (Boon Par and Boon Haw). Their father, Aw Chu Kin, started the family fortune in Rangoon, Burma, by selling "Tiger Balm" or *Ban Kim Ewe* (Chinese for Ten Thousand Golden Oil) as a poor man's panacea for all ailments.[43] The "Tiger Tycoon" then moved to Singapore in 1926 and shortly after, *Eng Aun Tong* was established in Neil Road. Today the building has been renovated for commercial use by Rosso/Cina.

Near Neil Road is Kampong Bahru [224] and the Church of St. Teresa at 510 Kampong Bahru Road [225 (*right, top*)]. The Church of St. Teresa resembles a miniature Notre Dome and was founded in 1929.

Neil Road also had many beautiful terrace houses [226] owned by well-to-do Peranakans. These houses were built in the 19th and 20th centuries: they have been dubbed Chinese Baroque, Palladian Chinese or Straits Chinese architecture – an eclectic combination of Chinese, Malay and European classical details.[5]

At the end of Neil Road was the Fairfield School [222; 223].

Tanjong Pagar Road and Keppel Road

Tanjong Pagar in Malay means "cape of stakes", a name which reflects its origin as a fishing village on a former promontory. The original name of Tanjong Pagar [227–230] is also said to be *Salinter*, a fishing village.[32] Keppel Road, which led to the harbour was built in 1886 and named after Admiral Sir Henry Keppel (1809–1904). Telok Blangah in Malay means "cooking pot bay" and it covers the area behind Keppel Harbour[32] [231].

Singapore General Hospital and Alexandra Hospital

New Bridge Road leads to Outram Road, and between Outram Road and Sepoy Lines lies the Singapore General Hospital. Its original building dates back to 1821; the present building was built in 1926 [232].

The Singapore General Hospital has been the main teaching hospital of the Medical School since it was founded on 3 July 1905 as the Straits and Federated Malay States Government Medical School.[44]

In 1946, after the Japanese Occupation, the three main blocks of the Singapore General Hospital (formerly known as Upper, Middle and Lower Blocks) were renamed Bowyer [233 (*right, middle*)], Stanley and Norris [234] Blocks respectively, in memory of the three medical officers (who had been closely associated with the hospitals of Singapore before the war) who had lost their lives during the Japanese Invasion.[45] The tower portion of Bowyer Block has been converted into the Singapore General Hospital Museum; it was opened by President S.R. Nathan on 20 May 2005 to coincide with the centenary of the Medical School (1905–2005). The Museum chronicles both the history of medicine in Singapore, and of the Singapore General Hospital.

Alexandra Hospital situated at Alexandra Road was first established in 1938 as a British Military Hospital [235] for the British in the Far East prior to the Second World War. In 1971, the hospital was handed over to the Singapore Government. When the Japanese invaded Singapore on 14–15 February 1942, many hospital staff and patients were massacred by the Japanese soldiers. Today, Alexandra Hospital is a flourishing restructured civilian hospital.

Church of St. Teresa around 1940.
(*See* [225])

The clock tower block of the Singapore General Hospital was named the Bowyer Block after the Japanese Occupation.
(*See* [233])

[164]

CHINESE TEMPLE. SINGAPORE.

Cancellation: 1901
Back: Undivided

This postcard depicts the Thian Hock Keng Temple on Telok Ayer Street around 1901.

[165]

SINGAPORE. SOUTH BRIDGE ROAD.

Cancellation: 1911
Back: Divided
Series and/or No.: 1556
Publisher: Wilson & Co., Orchard Road, Singapore

A view of the Thian Hock Keng Temple with Ann Siang Hill in the background. The postcard is wrongly captioned as "South Bridge Road".

[166]
CHINESE TEMPLE. SINGAPORE.

Cancellation: 1930
Back: Divided
Series and/or No.: 1012
Publisher: The Continental Stamp Company, Singapore

A colourful postcard of the Thian Hock Keng Temple on Telok Ayer Street around 1930.

[167]
CHINESE TEMPLE, TELUK AJER – SINGAPORE.
(C 1940)

Back: Divided

Mosquée à Singapore. Mohamedan Mosque, Singapore.

[168]
MOHAMEDAN MOSQUE, SINGAPORE. (c 1920)

Back: Divided
Publisher: Koh & Co., Singapore

Note the Palldian features on the street level and contrast them with the Islamic balustrades above.

MOHAMMEDAN TEMPLE, SINGAPORE.

[169]
MOHAMMEDAN TEMPLE, SINGAPORE. (c 1930)

Back: Undivided

[170]
Untitled [Telok Ayer Basin]. (c 1900)

Back: Divided

The Telok Ayer Basin is pictured with many boats and it is in the process of undergoing land reclamation.

[171]
TELOK AYE POLICE STATION. (C 1900)

Back: Divided

The old Telok Ayer Police Station at the corner of Cross and Market Streets, looking towards South Bridge Road. The station was demolished in 1957[4].

[172]
Untitled [The Telok Ayer Market]. (1904)
Cancellation: 1905
Back: Undivided

Octagonal in shape, the Telok Ayer Market is pictured with a small cupola at the centre of its roof.

INSIDE MARKET, SINGAPORE

[173]
INSIDE MARKET, SINGAPORE. (C 1930)
Back: Divided

This postcard depicts the cast iron interior structure of the Telok Ayer Market.

Singapore. Entrance to a Chinese House.

[174]

SINGAPORE. ENTRANCE TO A CHINESE HOUSE. (C 1900)

Cancellation: 1905
Back: Undivided

The Wak Hai Cheng Bio temple at Philip Street; its roof is decorated with a colourful array of porcelain figurines of people, animals and pagodas. There is a large open courtyard in front of the temple. The postcard has been mislabelled as "Entrance to a Chinese House".

Chinese Hotel   Singapore.

[175]

CHINESE HOTEL/SINGAPORE. (C 1900)

Back: Undivided

Depicts a hotel that is likely to be in the vicinity of Chinatown; its exact name and location are unknown.

[176]
JINRIKISHA QUARTERS, SINGAPORE. (C 1920)
Back: Divided

The scene is that of Sago Lane, with many rickshaws by the roadside.

[177]
CHINESE TOWN, SINGAPORE. (C 1930)
Back: Divided

Presenting Temple Street; notice the profusion of laundry hanging from poles protruding into the street on both sides.

[178]
RICKSHAW COOLIE QUARTERS, SINGAPORE. (1938)

Cancellation: 1938
Back: Divided

Depicting a typical morning marketing scene with many roadside sellers and buyers, and a solitary rickshaw with its puller.

[179]
CHINA TOWN SINGAPORE. (C 1940)

Cancellation: 1949
Back: Divided

A view of China Street; a rickshaw and a motorcar can be seen on the street.

[180]
RICKSHAW PULLER, SINGAPORE. (C 1920)

Back: Divided
Series and/or No.: 1076
Publisher: The Continental Stamp Company, Singapore

In this postcard, a rickshaw puller is taking a rest and having a meal at a roadside hawker stall.

[181]
Untitled [A rickshaw puller and his rickshaw]. (c 1930)

Back: Divided

A bare-chested rickshaw puller wearing a large straw hat working under the hot sun.

[182]

CHINESE SMOKING OPIUM. (C 1920)

Back: Divided

This postcard shows a bare-chested opium addict sleeping on a hard porcelain pillow, exposing his cachexic body and prominent ribs.

[183]

SINGAPORE. CHINESE OPIUM SMOKERS. (C 1930)

Back: Divided
Series and/or No.: 110
Publisher: Max H. Hilckes, Singapore

The two Chinese men lying on the bed are smoking opium while the other men sitting on the hardwood chairs are smoking water pipes.

Chinese Ayahs, Singapore.

[184]
CHINESE AYAHS, SINGAPORE. (C 1920)

Back: Divided
Publisher: German

Chinese servants wearing *samfoos* and trousers, carrying their masters' babies.

Chinese Women to Market, Singapore.

[185]
CHINESE WOMEN TO MARKET, SINGAPORE. (C 1938)

Cancellation: 1938
Back: Divided

A photographic postcard of Chinese *amahs* (servants) with pigtails going marketing in Chinatown. These *amahs* were often Cantonese and wore white *samfoos* and black trousers.

Chinese Coolies, Singapore.

[186]
CHINESE COOLIES, SINGAPORE. (C 1910)

Back: Divided

Showing Chinese coolies (labourers) pulling and pushing a two-wheel cart.

Ballast for road repairing, Singapore.

[187]
BALLAST FOR ROAD REPAIRING, SINGAPORE.
(C 1920)

Back: Divided
Publisher: Russian

Samsui women working at a road construction site. They are wearing large straw hats on top of their headgear.

Street Kuli

Chinese Rice Cake seller.

[188]
STREET KULI. (C 1910)

Back: Divided
Publisher: G.R. Lambert & Co., Singapore

[189]
CHINESE RICE CAKE SELLER. (C 1910)

Back: Divided
Publisher: G.R. Lambert & Co., Singapore

A Malay patron squatting in front of a Chinese
rice cake seller.

[190]
CHINESE SELLING PORK, SINGAPORE. (C 1910)

Back: Divided
Publisher: German

Two Chinese selling pork by the roadside.

[191]
VEGETABLE MARKET SINGAPORE. (1917)

Cancellation: 1917
Back: Divided
Publisher: Russian

Depicts a scene of a vegetable market in Chinatown with vegetable sellers by the side of the road.

Chinese Barber   Chinese Seller of Cold Drinks

[192]
CHINESE BARBER/CHINESE SELLER OF COLD DRINKS. (C 1902).

Cancellation: 1902
Back: Undivided

Chinese barbers were at that time itinerant barbers who travelled from house to house.

Trompan (a kind of clogs) seller, Singapore.

[193]
TROMPAN (A KIND OF CLOGS) SELLER, SINGAPORE. (1918)

Cancellation: 1918
Back: Divided

A travelling tradesman selling clogs in front of a row of dilapidated shophouses.

[194]

SINGAPORE. CHINESE ACTOR. (1908)

Cancellation: 1908
Back: Divided

[195]

CHINESE ACTOR & ACTRESS, SINGAPORE. (C 1910)

Back: Divided
Publisher: Koh & Co., Singapore

A Chinese actor and actress appearing in an opera entitled "Meeting the Fox (Vixen)" (written in the three Chinese characters at the top).

[196]
Untitled [Central Police Station and the Police Court]. (1898)

Cancellation: 1900
Back: Undivided
Publisher: Not stated. Attributed to Kunzli Freres, Zurich

South Bridge Road in 1898 showing the Central Police Station (left hand side) and the Police Court (right hand side). The building within the circular outline is the Raffles Museum and Library. A horse carriage is in the foreground.

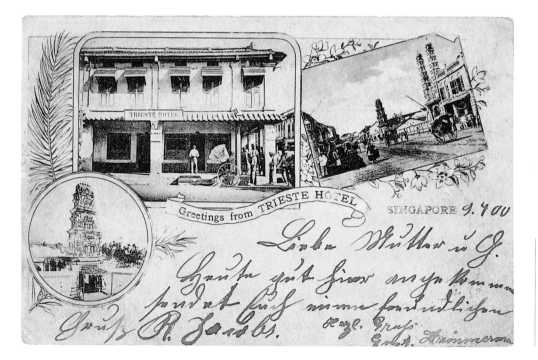

[197]
GREETINGS FROM TRIESTE HOTEL/SINGAPORE. (C 1900)

Cancellation: 1900
Back: Undivided

Shows the Trieste Hotel (believed to be in South Bridge Road) in the centre with the Jamae Mosque and Sri Mariamman Temple (right hand side) and the *gopuram* (gate tower) of the Sri Mariamman Temple (left hand side).

[198]
SINGAPORE, SOUTH BRIDGE ROAD. (1902)

Cancellation: 1902
Back: Undivided

Looking towards Maxwell Market showing the Jamae Mosque and the Sri Mariamman Temple. The Queen Victoria stamp affixed on the picture side of a postcard is not common.

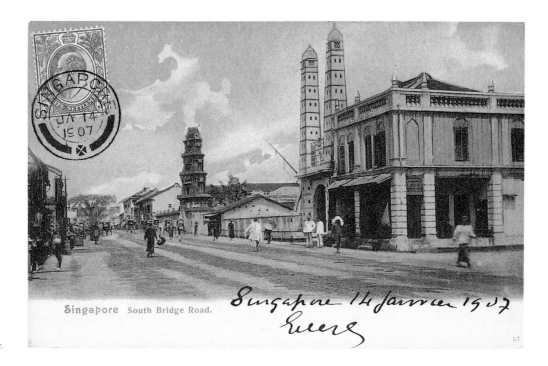

[199]
SINGAPORE SOUTH BRIDGE ROAD. (1907)

Cancellation: 1907
Back: Undivided

This postcard is similar to **[198]** but is in colour.

Singapore. Court House.

One of the main streets showing the court house & central police station

59

[200]

SINGAPORE. COURT HOUSE. (1904)

Cancellation: 1904
Back: Undivided

A view from South Bridge Road showing the Police Court (right hand side) and the Central Police Station (left hand side).

Singapore, Central Police Station.

[201]

SINGAPORE, CENTRAL POLICE STATION. (1922)

Cancellation: 1922
Back: Divided
Series and/or No.: 3030
Publisher: Max H. Hilckes, Singapore

The Police Court, Singapore.

[202]
THE POLICE COURT, SINGAPORE. (1926)

Cancellation: 1926
Back: Divided

The Police Court was demolished in 1977 and on the site was built the Hong Lim Shopping Centre.

[203]
STRAITS CHINESE RECREATION CLUB, SINGAPORE. (C 1910)

Back: Divided

Hong Lim Green with the octagonal pavilion of the Straits Chinese Recreation Club along South Bridge Road opposite the Central Police Station.

[204]
SOUTH BRIDGE ROAD, SINGAPORE.
(C 1920)

Cancellation: 1916
Back: Divided
Series and/or No.: 9150
Publisher: Russian

A busy scene of South Bridge Road with an electric tramway trolley bus, motor cars, rickshaws and bullock-carts on the road.

[205]
STREET SCENE, SINGAPORE. (C 1905)

Back: Divided

A view of Cross Street and its Chinese shops and Indian hawkers.

CROCKERY-WARE SHOPS, SINGAPORE.

[206]
CROCKERY-WARE SHOPS, SINGAPORE. (1911)

Cancellation: 1911
Back: Divided
Publisher: Koh & Co., Singapore

A rickshaw is parked outside a shop sellng pottery wares along Cross Street.

(16)   South Bridge Road, Singapore.

[207]
SOUTH BRIDGE ROAD, SINGAPORE. (c 1900)

Back: Divided

Cross Street, Singapore.

[208]
CROSS STREET, SINGAPORE. (C 1940)

Back: Divided
Publisher: Kong Hing Chiong & Co., North Bridge Road, Singapore

A view from Cross Street looking towards the Padang, with the dome of the Supreme Court visible in the background.

Hokien Street - SINGAPORE

[209]
HOKIEN STREET – SINGAPORE. (C 1920)

Back: Divided

A bullock-cart transporting goods and passengers along Hokein Street.

[210]
SINGAPORE. NEW BRIDGE ROAD. (1905)

Cancellation: 1905
Back: Undivided
Series and/or No.: 73

[211]
SINGAPORE. NEW BRIDGE ROAD. (1905)

Cancellation: 1905
Back: Undivided
Series and/or No.: 18

(13)   New Bridge Road, Singapore

[212]
NEW BRIDGE ROAD, SINGAPORE. (C 1910)

Back: Divided
Series and/or No.: 13

An early view of New Bridge Road; it was a deserted road with large Angsana trees by the road side.

130

New Bridge Road and its Bustling Communication Singapore.   No. 17

[213]
NEW BRIDGE ROAD AND ITS BUSTLING COMMUNICATION SINGAPORE. (C 1922)

Cancellation: 1922
Back: Divided

A bustling New Bridge Road crowded with bullock-carts, rickshaws and horse carriages.

Park Road, Singapore.

[214]
PARK ROAD, SINGAPORE. (1912)

Cancellation: 1912
Back: Divided
Publisher: Kong Hing Chiong & Co., North Bridge Road, Singapore

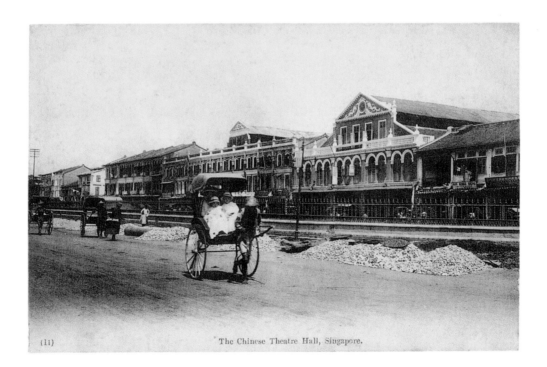

(11)   The Chinese Theatre Hall, Singapore.

[215]
THE CHINESE THEATRE HALL, SINGAPORE. (C 1920)

Back: Divided
Publisher: Russian

Shows the Heng Seng Peng and Heng Wai Sun Chinese opera theatre halls along Eu Tong Sen Street.

Chinese Protectorate, Singapore.

[216]
CHINESE PROTECTORATE, SINGAPORE. (1907)

Cancellation: 1907
Back: Divided
Publisher: German

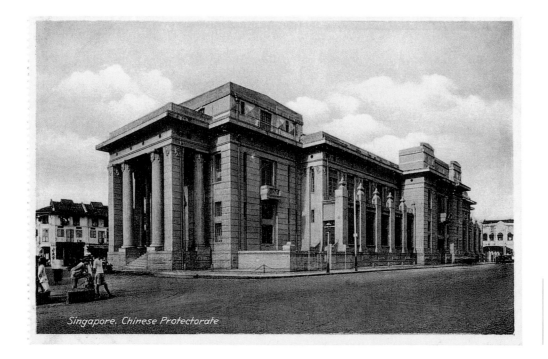

Singapore. Chinese Protectorate

[217]
SINGAPORE. CHINESE PROTECTORATE. (C 1930)

Back: Divided

It is now the Ministry of Labour Building; the building was gazetted as a national monument in 1998.

Singapore. Rail Road.

[218]
SINGAPORE. RAIL ROAD. (C 1914)

Cancellation: 1914
Back: Divided
Series and/or No.: 228
Publisher: Max H. Hilckes, Singapore

A view of Neil Road with the Jinricksha Station located on the left hand side.

South Bridge Road Jinrikisha Station, Singapore.

[219]
SOUTH BRIDGE ROAD JINRIKISHA STATION, SINGAPORE. (1915)

Cancellation: 1915
Back: Divided
Publisher: Russian

The Jinricksha Station at the corner of Neil Road and Tanjong Pagar Road, as viewed from South Bridge Road. This building is still standing and houses a restaurant; the vacant land in the left foreground is now occupied by the Maxwell Market food centre.

[220]
Untitled [Eng Aun Tong (Tiger Balm Hall)].
(1927)

Cancellation: 1927
Back: Undivided

Shows the Tiger Balm Hall at the corner of Neil Road and Craig Road. This is a privately printed postcard to advertise "Tiger Balm".

[221]
Untitled [Haw Par's Postcard]. (c 1940)

Cancellation: 1943
Back: Divided

Featuring the *Eng Aun Tong* Building in Neil Road together with a leaping tiger, three jars of Tiger Balm and an aeroplane! This is also another privately printed postcard meant to advertise *Eng Aun Tong*.

[222]
FAIRFIELD SCHOOL, SINGAPORE. (C 1920)

Back: Divided
Publisher: Methodist Publishing House, Singapore

Students taking a group photograph on the ground floor and the balcony of the second floor.

[223]
FAIRFIELD GIRL'S SCHOOL, SINGAPORE. (C 1940)

Back: Divided

Road at Kampong Bharu

[224]
ROAD AT KAMPONG BHARU. (C 1900)

Back: Undivided

Publisher: Verl v. Max Ludiwig, Deutsche
Buchhandlung, Singapore

Singapore. Church of St. Teresa of the Child Jesus

[225]
SINGAPORE. CHURCH OF ST. TERESA OF THE
CHILD JESUS. (C 1940)

Back: Divided

A real photographic postcard of the Church of St.
Teresa with a serrated left border; this indicates
that it was torn from a postcard booklet.

[226]
CHINESE RESIDENCE, SINGAPORE. (C 1910)

Back: Divided

A terrace house in Neil Road belonging to a well-to-do Peranakan. Notice the two ceramic elephants guarding the entrance and the metal archway holding an ornate lamp.

[227]
SINGAPORE. TANJONG PAGAR POLICE STATION. (1910)

Cancellation: 1910
Back: Divided
Series and/or No.: 226
Publisher: Max H. Hilckes, Singapore

This building has since been demolished.

Tanjong Pagar Godown, Singapore.

[228]
TANJONG PAGAR GODOWN, SINGAPORE.
(C 1900).

Back: Divided
Publisher: Kong Hing Chiong & Co., 104 North
Bridge Road, Singapore

Singapore. Road to Tanjong Pagar.

19

[229]
SINGAPORE. ROAD TO TANJONG PAGAR. (C 1900)

Back: Divided

The building in the distance (right hand side) with
a cupola was the Tanjong Pagar Police Station.

TANJONG PAGAR ROAD.

[230]
TANJONG PAGAR ROAD. (C 1930)

Back: Undivided

The building on the postcard's left hand side was appropriately named "Virginia House" (visible on the arch near the roof) as it housed the American Tobacco Company (Straits) Ltd. The "Virginia" brand was a popular brand of cigarette in the 1920s and 1930s.

Teluk Blanja. Keppel Road to new Harbour Dock.

[231]
TELUK BLANJA. KEPPEL ROAD TO NEW HARBOUR DOCK. (1908)

Cancellation: 1908
Back: Undivided
Publisher: Hartwig & Co., Succ., Singapore

[232]

GENERAL HOSPITAL & GOAL. (C 1900)

Cancellation: 1905
Back: Undivided

The Outram Prison is located in the background (right hand side) and the grass patch in front of the hospital was used as a golf course!

[233]

SINGAPORE GENERAL HOSPITAL. (C 1930)

Back: Divided

The clock tower block was named the Bowyer Block in 1946 after a Dr. Bowyer who died during the Japanese Invasion. Since 20 May 2005, the Tower of Bowyer Block houses the Singapore General Hospital Museum.

[234]
GENERAL HOSPITAL S'PORE. (C 1940)

Cancellation: 1954
Back: Divided
Series and/or No.: M14

A photographic postcard of the Singapore General Hospital's Norris Block.

M 14. GENERAL HOSPITAL S'PORE

[235]
BRITISH MILITARY HOSPITAL, ALEXANDER S'PORE. (C 1940)

Back: Undivided

A photographic picture postcard of the British Military Hospital at Alexandra Road. The Royal Coat of Arms can be seen on top of the porch at the main entrance. In 1971, it became the Alexandra Hospital, a civilian hospital under the Ministry of Health, Singapore.

D 42   BRITISH MILITARY HOSPITAL, ALEXANDER S'PORE.

BEACH ROAD and VICINITY

A view of Clyde Terrace Market taken from the sea-side around 1920.
(*See* [242])

The Chinese Gospel Hall, North Bridge Road, in 1911.
(*See* [250])

Beach Road

Beach Road [236; 237] is one of the earliest roads developed in Singapore; it was a coastal road fronting the sea coast. For many years, Beach Road ran parallel to the seashore. Together with Robinson Road, Collyer Quay and the Esplanade, they formed one of the main east-west arteries of the town.[5,32] The Chinese used to call Beach Road *thih pa sat khau* (meaning the street to which the iron market faces), a reference to the Clyde Terrace Market [241-243] (*left, top*), a public market in 1910. The road was also formerly known to the Chinese as *ji chap keng* or "twenty houses street" – an allusion to the large garden bungalow houses fronting the sea in the early 19th century.[32] In 1886, one such house was converted into what is known today as the Raffles Hotel.

The first reclamation of the sea alongside Beach Road (Raffles Reclamation) started in 1843 and it provided land to build the Alhambra and Marlborough cinemas [240], a police station, the Singapore Volunteer Corps, Straits Settlements Volunteer Force Headquarters [239] and Drill Hall [238] (now known as the Singapore Infantry Requirement Headquarters).[32,47] The idea of a Volunteer Corps for Singapore was first mooted in 1846; the success of the Singapore Volunteer Artillery inspired other Volunteer Corps to be formed: collectively they became known as the Singapore Volunteer Corps with its headquarters situated at Beach Road.[47] Drill Hall was originally built at Fort Fullerton in 1891 and later transported to the Beach Road Headquarters and remained there from 1908 to 1933.[47]

The Marlborough and Alhambra cinemas were demolished in 1976 and on its site was built Shaw Towers.[9] Beach Lane was built on reclaimed land opposite the junction of Rochor Road and Beach Road as was shown in a prewar map.[46]

North Bridge Road

North and South Bridge Roads [244-249] were some of the earliest roads in Singapore; they ran across the north and the south of Elgin Bridge over the Singapore River; hence the names. The Chinese referred to the North Bridge Road area as *sio poh* (small town).[32]

The Chinese Gospel Hall [250 (*left, middle*)] was built in 1866 at North Bridge Road. The Church was destroyed in a Japanese air raid in 1941; after the war, a new Gospel Hall was built in Geylang.[48] The Hokkien called it *Hok Im Koan*; in 1916 it held Hokkien Prayer Meeting and Malay-Baba services weekly.

The Singapore Malay Theatre [251] was situated at North Bridge Road in the vicinity where Parco-Bugis Junction/Blanco Court stands today.[37]

The Union Jack Club was a residential club for members of the British Armed Services; it was formed in 1904. In Singapore, the first Union Jack Club was opposite the Raffles Hotel.[49] In 1924, a new Union Jack Club was built on North Bridge Road [252] in the vicinity of Capitol Theatre.[37] It was demolished in the early 1970s following the British withdrawal from Singapore, and was never rebuilt.

The Masjid Sultan (Sultan Mosque) [253] is situated at 3 Muscat Street (Pedestrian Street) at the corner of North Bridge Road and Arab Street; it was gazetted a national monument in 1975. "The mosque is an enduring testimony to the munificence of Sultan Hussein who was present with Sir Stamford Raffles at the founding of Singapore, and of his descendants... He built the first mosque on this spot. When the mosque approached its centenary, part of the old mosque was demolished and a larger one was built... The new Masjid Sultan, like the old, was supported by Muslims of all communities: Malay, Bugis, Arab and Indian."[30]

Malay Street, Hylam Street and Middle Road

In the prewar days, Malay Street [254; 255] was the most notorious street in Singapore – it was the prostitute den of Chinese, Japanese and European ladies [256; 257]. Malay Street and Hylam Street were part of "Little Japan", which begun as far back as 1877 with *karayuki-san* (Japanese prostitutes).[50] The number of shops for *karayuki-san* increased [258; 260; 261] and "Little Japan" flourished.

Sometime in 1932, the "red light area" was officially banned.[51] During its heyday, the notorious Malay Street was the ultimate fantasy for lonely bachelors wanting a taste of the lurid East.[50] Prostitution in prewar Singapore has been well-described by Yvonne Quah (1986).[51]

Since the opening of Parco Bugis Junction Shopping complex in 1995, Malay Street along with Hylam Street and Malabar Street has been incorporated within the new shopping mall as an indoor air-conditioned "indoor street".[32]

Middle Road was part of "Little Japan" in the prewar days; a famous Japanese departmental store there was *Echigoya*.[46] In 1879, Father Jose Pedro de Cunha of St. Joseph Church (a Portuguese Mission) started a school for poor parishioners in Middle Road (St. Anna's School); in 1886 the school became known as St. Anthony's Boys' and Girls' School. In 1906, the school became known as St. Anthony's Convent[52] [262]. In 1995, both the primary and secondary schools of St. Anthony's Convent moved into their new premises at Bedok North Avenue 4.[52]

Victoria Street

Victoria Street [270] was named after Queen Victoria (1819–1901). The Chinese called the street *au bei chia lo* (back of horse carriage street) i.e. the back of North Bridge Road.

The most prominent structure along Victoria Street is the towering spire of the chapel of the Convent of the Holy Infant Jesus (CHIJ) [263]. Father Jean-Marie Beurel, the founder of the Cathedral of the Good Shepherd and St. Joseph's Institution, had bought the charming house opposite the Cathedral, which G.D. Coleman had built for H.C. Caldwell, a magistrate's clerk. In this house in 1852, Father Beurel started the Convent of the Holy Infant Jesus.[30] The convent [264-267] also housed boarders and an orphanage.

The grand Anglo-French Gothic chapel was designed by Father Charles Benedict Nain, a priest in the St. Peter and Paul's Church. The construction of the chapel was completed in 1903; a five-storey spire flanked by flying buttresses marked the entrance to the chapel. Today, the chapel with its towering spire has been restored and preserved as "CHIJMES": a flourishing centre of fine restaurants and shops.[53]

The Victoria School was founded in 1876; it has moved five times since its first campus in Kampong Glam; its Tyrwhitt and Syed Alwi (Victoria Bridge) campus is shown [269 (*right, top*)] around 1917. This "Victoria Bridge School, Singapore" is featured on the reverse side of Singapore's current $2 currency bill.[54] Its present campus at Siglap Link in Marine Parade was opened in 2003.[54]

The Straits and Federated Malay States Government Medical School had an outpatient maternity department in the Maternity Hospital at Victoria Street [268].[44]

High Street, Hill Street, Coleman Street and Armenian Street

High Street [271; 272 (*right, middle*)] is probably the oldest street in Singapore. It was so named as it is on topographically high ground. Up till the 1960s, High Street [273-277], together with Raffles Place, were the centres of Singapore's upmarket retail sector before they were superseded by Orchard Road. It was also the site of several buildings owned by the Indian community. It is today referred to by the Hokkiens as *tua kok koi* which means "Supreme Court Street."[32]

An earlier campus of Victoria School (Tyrwhitt and Syed Alwi Victoria Bridge Campus) in 1917. (*See* [269])

Junction of High Street and North Bridge Road around 1916. (*See* [272])

Anglo-Chinese School Singapore, Coleman Street, around 1910.
(*See* [283])

The canal along Stamford Road (c 1915) being lined by large shady trees.
(*See* [289])

Whiteaway Laidlaw & Co. [279] was a prominent departmental store in the prewar era. "European residents in Asia owe a debt of gratitude to such pioneer concern as Messrs Whiteaway, Laidlaw & Co.; who has branches in almost every Eastern city. The Singapore firm was established in 1900 in D'Almeida Street. It removed to its imposing quarters at the corner of Hill Street and Stamford Road..."[18] The building on Hill Street was built [279] in 1904; it was used by the company till 1910 when it moved to Fullerton Square. In 1933, the building was converted to the Oranjie Hotel [286; 287]. After the Second World War, it was renamed the Stamford House in 1963[4] and was occupied by MPH (Malayan Publishing House).

The Central Fire Station [280; 281] at 62 Hill Street is a striking red and white building in the Neo-Classical style architecture. It began operations in 1908 and it represented a major step towards modern and efficient fire-fighting; in the previous century, fires were dealt with by volunteers and men from the police and military forces. The Hill Street Central Fire Station was fitted with residential quarters and garages for motorised engines. It had a central watchtower [280] from which to look out for fires but this was also used for drying out hoses.[30]

Before the war, the prominent buildings on Coleman Street were the Adelphi Hotel, the Hotel de la Paix [282] and the Anglo-Chinese School [283 (*left, top*)]. The school was founded on 1 March 1886 by Bishop William Oldham and served as an extension of the Methodist Church. The name of the school came from the fact that it conducted lessons in English in the mornings and Chinese in the afternoons.[55] In the 1980s, the front building of the school was occupied by the Methodist Book Room. When the school vacated its premises in 1992, the main portion of the school was taken over by the National Archives of Singapore. The Methodist Book Room was taken over by the Telecoms Authority of Singapore in 1993 and in August 1995, it reopened (after

extensive renovation) as the Singapore Philatelic Museum at 23B Coleman Street.

Armenian Street [285] derived its name from the Armenian Church located there. The Bible House [284] could be viewed from the garden wall of the Armenian Church; it existed till the 1970s before it was demolished and the Bible Society of Singapore was built. The Tao Nan School [285] was built in 1910–1912 in the Neo-Classical style. It had been set up by the Singapore Hokkien Association in 1906. However, the school moved to Marine Parade in 1976 and in 1999, the building was reopened as the Asian Civilisations Museum; the building was gazetted a national monument in 1998.[53]

Stamford Road and Fort Canning Road

Stamford Road [290] was named after the founder of Singapore, Sir Stamford Raffles. The Chinese called it *lau chui khe* or "flowing water road" for at high tide, the Stamford Canal [289 (*left, middle*); 291] overflowed its banks. It was also formerly known as Hospital Street.[32] The Hotel Van Wijk was also located at Stamford Road [288].

The Capitol Theatre [292] was built by the Namazie brothers in 1929; the building was known as "Namazie Mansions". Initially a cabaret, it became a cinema in 1946; it screened its last movie in 1998.[53] The Raffles Library and Museum [293-297; 308] was conceived in 1849; the building at the corner of Stamford Road and Fort Canning Road was officially opened in 1887 during the Diamond Jubilee Year of Queen Victoria. It was designed by the colonial engineer, Sir Henry McCallum; it is Neo-Palladian and Renaissance in style. In 1960, its name was changed to the National Museum; in the 1980s the name was further changed to Singapore History Museum and it was also gazetted as a national monument.[53] It closed in 2004 for extensive renovation and expansion and when it reopens in 2006/2007 it will have more than doubled its exhibition space.

Fort Canning Road was named after Viscount Canning, the Governor-General of India from 1859 to 1861. Along this road is the Wesley Methodist Church and its Parsonage [298; 300]. The church's site had been a gift from the colonial government to the Methodist Mission in appreciation of its social and educational contributions. The church is shaped like a cross and features stained glass windows and brick facings.[53]

Bras Basah Road

Bras Basah means "wet rice" in Malay; in the early days, wet rice was exposed to the sun on the banks of the Sungei Bras Basah (Stamford Canal). The road was also called Church Street and College Street because of the large number of schools and churches in the vicinity.[5] Two prominent buildings along Bras Basah Road are the Cathedral of the Good Shepherd and St. Joseph's Institution [301]. Founded by Father Beurel and designed by Denis Lesley McSwiney, the church [304-306] was consecrated on 6 June 1846. Inside the church is a statue of Jesus carrying a lamb; the inscription below it reads "I am the Good Shepherd."[53]

St. Joseph's Institution [302 (*right, top*); 303] was first erected in 1852 on Bras Basah Road. The present building was erected in 1867 and further extended in 1903 and 1905 until the school chapel was constructed in 1911. In 1992, the building was gazetted as a national monument and was converted into the Singapore Art Museum, which opened on 20 December 1996.[53]

The Caledonian Hotel [307] at Bras Basah Road was converted into the Japanese Commercial Museum and the Student House occupied the second floor.[5,46] The Bethesda [299] was a church on Bras Basah Road (in the vicinity of Carlton Hotel)[35]; it was demolished in the postwar years. It first started out as a wooden structure known as the Bethesda Hall on 30 September 1866; a few years later, the building was destroyed by white ants. In 1892, a new Bethesda church was erected; a

year later the Bethesda Mission House was added behind the church.

The Ladies Lawn Tennis Club [310] was located on the playing field along Bras Basah Road facing the Cathay Cinema; it belonged to the YWCA (Young Women's Christian Association) [309]; this was its second club[9]; its first club was in Penang Lane.[57] At the northern end of Bras Basah Road at its junction with Dhoby Ghaut was the Lois Molteni Confectionery [312]; the site is presently occupied by the Cathay Building [313], which was Singapore's first skyscraper. Built in 1939, it was designed by Frank Brewer and owned by the Loke family. When Singapore surrendered to the Japanese on 15 February 1942, General Percival flew the Japanese flag from the top of Cathay Building to signal the surrender of the British. The cinema closed down in 2000.[53]

Selegie Road, Sophia Road and Mount Sophia

Selegie Road [311] could have been named after a Bugis pirate chief (Orang Selegie), or after a wooden spear or nibong palm.[32] Sophia Road [259; 315] and Mount Sophia were named after Lady Sophia, the second wife of Sir Stamford Raffles; the name could however also refer to Mary Sophia Anne (1823–1858), daughter of Captain William Flint, Sir Stamford's brother-in-law.[32] The Methodist Girls' School [314] was on Short Street (opposite Selegie Road).

Eu Villa (*right, middle*) at Mount Sophia was one of the most magnificent and opulent private residences ever built in Singapore; it was demolished in the 1970s. It was originally built in 1915 for the Penang-born millionaire, Eu Tong Sen; it was built in the Edwardian Baroque style and had ten bedrooms, a Renaissance dome over the entrance hall and steeples over the dressing rooms on the first floor.[58] It cost $1 million in furnishings alone; the handsome furniture was imported from Paris and London while the marble statues were fine examples of Florentine art.[33]

Bras Basah Road in 1912, with St. Joseph's School on the right hand side.
(*See* [302])

Aerial view of Eu Tong Sen's House at Mount Sophia around 1940.

Beach Road, Singapore

[236]
BEACH ROAD, SINGAPORE. (C 1910)

Back: Divided
Series and/or No.: 1013
Publisher: The Continental Stamp Company,
Singapore

Adjacent to Raffles Hotel (the roof of which is
just visible on right next to the large tree), the
two buildings have Palladian-style windows;
these were built in 1901 (the date is just visible
above the second-storey window).

BEACH ROAD
SINGAPORE
NO.229

[237]
BEACH ROAD SINGAPORE. (C 1920)

Back: Divided
Series and/or No.: 229

A closer view of one of the two blocks of
buildings shown in **[236]**; it is now occupied by
"The Miyako Hotel" (the name is just visible on
the ground floor, to the left of the loaded
bullock-cart).

[238]
S.V.C. Drill Hall, Singapore. (c 1920)
Back: Divided

A real photographic postcard showing the Singapore Volunteer Corps Drill Hall.

[239]
S.S.V.F. Head Quarters, Singapore. (c 1930)
Back: Undivided

The Straits Settlements Volunteer Force Headquarters is shown here at Beach Road.

ALHAMBRA CINEMA HALL, SINGAPORE.

[240]
ALHAMBRA CINEMA HALL, SINGAPORE. (C 1930)
Back: Divided

This photographic postcard shows the Alhambra Cinema Hall (left hand side) and the Marlborough Cinema Hall (right hand side) in the 1930s. Between the two cinema halls is the signboard "Home of Paramount Pictures". Both cinema halls were demolished in 1976.

148

H. Grimaud - Mohamed Yahya - Singapour
SINGAPOUR (Indes) - Marché Couvert

[241]
SINGAPOUR (INDES) – MARCHE CONVERT.
[CLYDE TERRACE MARKET, SINGAPORE.]
(C 1900)

Cancellation: 1916
Back: Divided
Publisher: H. Grimaud, Mohamed Yahya, Singapore

The Clyde Terrace Market on Clyde Terrace/Beach Lane.

[242]
CLYDE TERRACE MARKET. SINGAPORE. (C 1920)

Back: Divided
Publisher: Koh & Co., Singapore

A view of Clyde Terrace Market taken from the sea-side; fishing boats can be seen in the foreground.

[243]
BEACH ROAD SINGAPORE. (C 1930)

Back: Divided
Publisher: G.H. Kiat & Co., Singapore

Clyde Terrace Market being visible from Beach Road; many rickshaws and a few cars are parked alongside the market.

North Bridge Road.

[244]
NORTH BRIDGE ROAD. (C 1900)

Back: Undivided

The road is empty except for two rickshaws and itinerant hawkers.

(5)   North Bridge Road, Singapore

[245]
NORTH BRIDGE ROAD, SINGAPORE. (C 1910)

Back: Divided
Publisher: Russian

A view of North Bridge Road looking towards High Street; the railings on the left mark the boundary of St. Andrew's Cathedral.

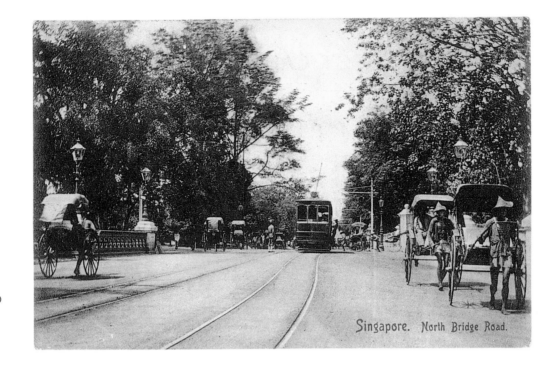

Singapore. North Bridge Road.

[246]
SINGAPORE. NORTH BRIDGE ROAD. (C 1910)

Back: Divided
Publisher: Koh & Co., Singapore

An electric tram and rickshaws plying North Bridge Road

North Bridge Road, Singapore

[247]
NORTH BRIDGE ROAD, SINGAPORE. (C 1920)

Back: Divided
Series and/or No.: S 97

North Bridge Road at its junction with Bras Basah Road; the Medical Hall (the building with a big red cross on top) used to be a prominent landmark till its demolition in the 1980s.

[248]

NORTH BRIDGE ROAD, SINGAPORE. (C 1930)

Back: Divided

A real photographic postcard of North Bridge Road; the road was crowded with a trolley bus, cars, rickshaws, bullock-carts and pedestrians. A tailor shop, silk store and goldsmith shop are discernible on the postcard's right hand side.

[249]

NORTH BRIDGE SINGAPORE. (C 1940)

Back: Divided

The building on the postcard's right hand side housed the "Tiong Hua" hotel and the "Lian Tian" Club while the building on the left was the Meyer's Mansions (at Coleman Street corner).

[250]

CHINESE MISSION, SINGAPORE. (1911)

Cancellation: 1911
Back: Divided
Publisher: German

The Chinese Gospel Hall in North Bridge Road; a bullock-drawn watering cart is in front of it.

[251]

MALAY THEATRE SINGAPORE. (C 1910)

Cancellation: 1916
Back: Divided

The Singapore Malay Theatre at North Bridge Road; the postcard has a serrated left border (it was torn from a postcard booklet).

[252]

SINGAPORE. (C 1940)

Back: Divided

A photographic postcard of the Union Jack Club at North Bridge Road; the name of the club is visible at the entrance below the flag (postcard's right hand side); the year it was built (1924) is etched at the foot of the flag pole.

[253]

MOSLEM MOSQUE S'PORE. (C 1940)

Cancellation: 1950
Back: Undivided

A photographic postcard of the Masjid Sultan (Sultan Mosque) at the corner of North Bridge Road and Arab Street.

[254]

MALAY STREET, SINGAPORE. (c 1930)

Back: Divided

This is a view of Malay Street; many of the shops on the right were Japanese prostitute dens.

[255]

HYLAM STREET, SINGAPORE. (c 1930)

Back: Divided

The Japanese photographer's shop (S.T. Yamato) is visible on the right hand side and a big Japanese kite in the form of a fish is on its left hand side. Hylam Street also had many Japanese prostitute dens in the prewar days.

[256]
SINGAPORE. JAPANESE LADY. (1907)

Cancellation: 1907
Back: Divided

A Japanese lady who was most likely to be
residing in the Malay Street area (Little Japan).

[257]
JAPANESE GIRL, SINGAPORE. (C 1930)

Back: Divided

A posed photograph of a Japanese lady sitting on
a bench in the vicinity of Malay Street.

"FUJI" JAPANESE RESTAURANT
3 Malay Street SINGAPORE

Panorama of Sophia Road, Singapore.

[258]
"FUJI" JAPANESE RESTAURANT/3 MALAY STREET
SINGAPORE. (C 1920)

Back: Divided

This postcard also has a serrated left border (it was detached from a menu card). It depicts a beautiful Japanese lady. The restaurant was also a prostitute den.

[259]
PANORAMA OF SOPHIA ROAD, SINGAPORE. (C 1910)

Back: Undivided

This is a colour-tinted postcard which depicts a bungalow at Sophia Road in the early 1900s.

"FUJI" JAPANESE RESTAURANT
3 Malay Street SINGAPORE

[260]
FUJI FROM SHOJI LAKE/"FUJI" JAPANESE
RESTAURANT/3 MALAY STREET SINGAPORE.
(C 1920)
Back: Divided

"FUJI" JAPANESE RESTAURANT
3 Malay Street SINGAPORE.

[261]
VIEW OF MIYAJIMA/"FUJI" JAPANESE
RESTAURANT/3 MALAY STREET SINGAPORE
[AN ADVERTISEMENT FOR FUJI RESTAURANT].
(C 1920)
Back: Divided

This Japanese postcard was used to advertise the
Fuji Restaurant; the restaurant was also used as a
Japanese prostitute den. The postcard has a
serrated lower border (it was detached from the
top of a menu card).

[262]
ST. ANTHONY'S CONVENT, SINGAPORE.
(c 1910)

Back: Divided

A photographic postcard of the building, which
housed St. Anthony's Convent.

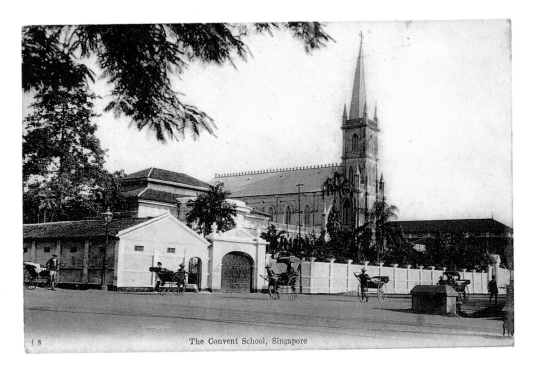

[263]
THE CONVENT SCHOOL, SINGAPORE. (c 1910)

Back: Divided
Series and/or No.: 8
Publisher: Russian

The towering spire of its chapel clearly
dominated Victoria Street.

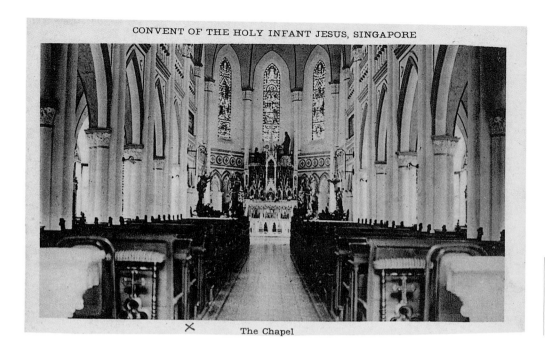

CONVENT OF THE HOLY INFANT JESUS, SINGAPORE

The Chapel

[264]
CONVENT OF THE HOLY INFANT JESUS,
SINGAPORE/THE CHAPEL. (C 1920)

Back: Divided

Depicts the interior of the Chapel of the Convent
of the Holy Infant Jesus; the stained glass
windows are clearly visible in the centre.

CONVENT OF THE HOLY INFANT JESUS, SINGAPORE

The Boarders'refectory

[265]
CONVENT OF THE HOLY INFANT JESUS,
SINGAPORE/THE BOARDERS' REFECTORY.
(C 1920)

Back: Divided
Publisher: Aulard, Iung et Cie, 6, Rue-du Vieux-
Colombier, Paris

The Boarders' Refectory (dining room) of the
Convent of the Holy Infant Jesus showing a nun
serving bread.

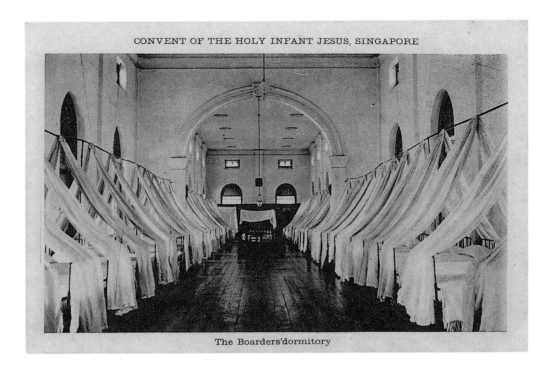

CONVENT OF THE HOLY INFANT JESUS, SINGAPORE

The Boarders' dormitory

[266]
CONVENT OF THE HOLY INFANT JESUS,
SINGAPORE/THE BOARDERS' DORMITORY.
(C 1920)

Back: Divided
Publisher: Aulard, Iung et Cie, 6, Rue-du Vieux-
Colombier, Paris

The Boarders' dormitory in the Convent of the
Holy Infant Jesus; all the beds had conspicuous
mosquito nets.

VICTORIA ST
SINGAPORE

[267]
VICTORIA ST SINGAPORE. (C 1928)

Back: Divided

A couple of dental shops are visible on the
postcard's right hand side while the chapel of the
convent is clearly seen on its left. The postcard
was written but not posted.

The Straits Medical School, Singapore

[268]
THE STRAITS MEDICAL SCHOOL, SINGAPORE.
(C 1920)

Back: Divided
Series and/or No.: 31
Publisher: Koh & Co., Singapore

The caption on this ppc is inaccurate; it showed the Maternity Hospital in 1913 at Victoria Street (where the Straits and Federated Malay States Government Medical School had an outpatient maternity department).

Victoria Bridge School, Singapore

[269]
VICTORIA BRIDGE SCHOOL, SINGAPORE. (1917)

Cancellation: 1917
Back: Divided
Series and/or No.: 26
Publisher: Koh & Co., Singapore

An earlier campus of Victoria School (Tyrwhitt and Syed Alwi Victoria Bridge Campus).

Victoria Street, Singapore

[270]
VICTORIA STREET, SINGAPORE. (C 1910)

Back: Divided
Series and/or No.: 77
Publisher: Russian

A view of Victoria Street at its junction with Stamford Road; part of the Hotel van Wijk can be seen on the postcard's right hand side.

Singapore. ∅.8.2.02. High-Street mit dem Hôtel Europe.

[271]
SINGAPORE. HIGH-STREET MIT DEM HOTEL EUROPE. (1902)

Cancellation: 1902
Back: Undivided
Publisher: Ludwig & Ressel's Reisebuchanallung, Singapore

Presenting a view of High Street; on the postcard's right hand side is the Hotel de l'Europe; in the distance is Fort Canning (Government Hill) with its lighthouse.

[272]
JUNCTION OF HIGH STREET & NORTH BRIDGE ROAD, SINGAPORE. (1916)

Cancellation: 1916
Back: Divided
Series and/or No.: 6
Publisher: Russian

An electric tram turning into High Street from North Bridge Road; Elgin Bridge can be seen at the far end of North Bridge Road.

[273]
HIGH STREET, SINGAPORE. (C 1920)

Back: Divided

A view of High Street looking towards the Padang with the Hotel de l'Europe on the postcard's left hand side, and many shops on both sides of the street; the firm of G.H. Kiat & Co. is clearly visible on its right hand side.

[274]
HIGH STREET, SINGAPORE. (C 1920)

Back: Divided

A large Union Jack is fluttering prominently; shops signs visible include "Jewellers", "Silk Merchants" and "Malacca Canes".

[275]
HIGH STREET, SINGAPORE. (C 1940)

Back: Divided

High Street overlooking Fort Canning; the shop signs that are readable from the postcard include Assomull & Co., Singapore Photo Co., J.C.M. etc.

[276]
TRAFFIC POLICE, SINGAPORE. (1934)

Cancellation: 1934
Back: Divided

The signboard "Quan Seng/Photographers" is visible to the right of the traffic policeman with rattan wings.

[277]
KIYONO & CO.

Back: Divided

A real photographic multiview picture postcard with four views of the Japanese firm Kiyono & Co., a Malacca cane company. It was located at 2 High Street.

[278]
HILL STREET, SINGAPORE. (C 1905)

Back: Divided

The building on the postcard's right hand side is
the Masonic Hall.

[279]
HILL STREET, SINGAPORE. (C 1905)

Back: Divided
Series and/or No.: 70
Publisher: Russian

The building on the postcard's left hand side is
the famous departmental store, Messrs.
Whiteaway Laidlaw & Co. The company
occupied the building from 1904 to 1910.
In 1933 the building was converted into the
Oranjie Hotel.

[280]

HOCK LAM STREET SINGAPORE. (C 1940)

Back: Divided

A view of the Hill Street Fire Station's watchtower, as seen from Hock Lam Street. Hock Lam Street was expunged in the 1970s when Funan Centre was built over the site.

[281]

SINGAPORE FIRE BRIGADE. (C 1940)

Back: Divided

The Central Fire Station at 62 Hill Street with its prominent watch tower. The living quarters of the firemen are depicted on the postcard's right hand side.

Hotel de la Paix, Singapore.

[282]
HOTEL DE LA PAIX, SINGAPORE. (1909)

Cancellation: 1909
Back: Divided

The Hotel de la Paix became the Burlington Hotel prior to the Second World War; in the 1970s it was demolished and replaced by the Peninsula Hotel.

Anglo-Chinese School, Singapore.

[283]
ANGLO-CHINESE SCHOOL, SINGAPORE. (C 1910)

Back: Divided
Publisher: Methodist Publishing House, Singapore

THE BIBLE HOUSE, SINGAPORE.

303   ARMENIAN ST. SINGAPORE

[284]
THE BIBLE HOUSE, SINGAPORE. (C 1910)

Back: Divided

A view of the Bible House taken from the
back garden wall of the Armenian Church.
The building was demolished in the 1970s.

[285]
ARMENIAN ST. SINGAPORE. (C 1940)

Back: Divided

A photographic postcard of Armenian Street
looking towards St Joseph's Institution. The Tao
Nan School is on the postcard's left hand side.

ORANJE HOTEL—SINGAPORE.

[286]
ORANJE HOTEL – SINGAPORE. (C 1935)

Back: Divided

This postcard is pink in colour and has a serrated bottom (it had been detached from a menu card).

LOUNGE

ORANJE HOTEL
39 STAMFORD ROAD,
SINGAPORE.

BEDROOM

[287]
ORANJE HOTEL/39 STAMFORD ROAD/SINGAPORE. (C 1935)

Back: Divided

Contains three views of the hotel (the hotel from the outside is flanked by its lounge and a bedroom). This postcard is orange in colour

(15)   Raffles Museum & Library, Singapore

[288]
RAFFLES MUSEUM & LIBRARY. (1910)

Back: Divided

This postcard has been wrongly labelled; it is
actually a view of the Hotel Van Wijk from its
junction with Victoria Street.

Stamford Road, Singapore

[289]
STAMFORD ROAD, SINGAPORE. (C 1915)

Back: Divided
Publisher: Russian

Stamford Road with its canal and lined by large
shady trees.

[290]
STAMFORD ROAD AND CANAL, SINGAPORE.
(C 1920)

Back: Divided

[291]
THE CANAL SINGAPORE. (1924)

Cancellation: 1924
Back: Divided

A photo of the canal that ran parallel to Stamford Road.

[292]
STAMFORD ROAD, SINGAPORE. (c 1940)
Back: Divided

A view of the Capitol Theatre at the junction of Stamford Road and North Bridge Road; the building is known as "Namazie Mansions"; the name is visible above the words "Capitol Theatre".

[293]
MUSEUM SINGAPORE. (1922)
Cancellation: 1922
Back: Divided

[294]
MUSEUM. (1900)

Cancellation: 1900
Back: Undivided

This postcard was sold by W. Winddrath, a well-known stamp dealer.

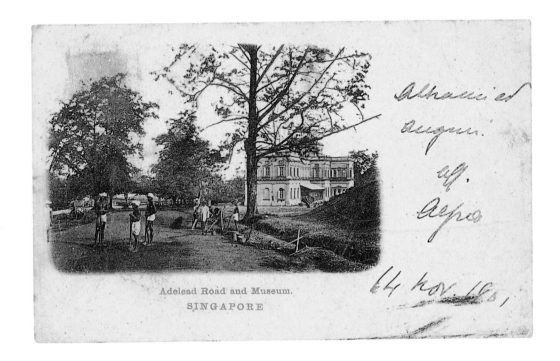

[295]
ADELEAD ROAD AND MUSEUM/SINGAPORE.
(1901)

Cancellation: 1901
Back: Undivided

No record of Adelead Road can be found in Singapore's history.

[296]

RAFFLES LIBRARY, SINGAPORE. (1925)

Cancellation: 1925
Back: Divided
Publisher: Kelly & Walsh Ltd, Singapore

The Raffles Library displaying its majestic dome; the Royal Coat of Arms in plaster is visible above the windows of the first floor.

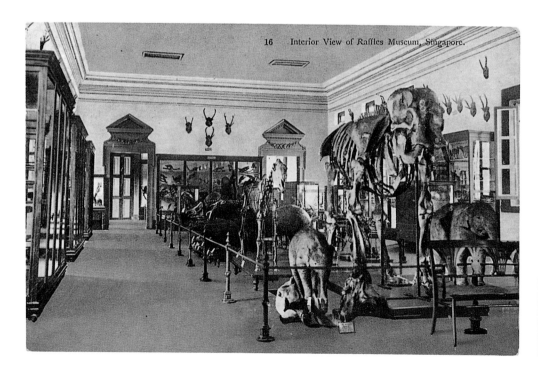

[297]

INTERIOR VIEW OF RAFFLES MUSEUM, SINGAPORE. (C 1930)

Series and/or No.: 16
Back: Divided

The museum also exhibited samples of fauna from the region.

Wolsey Methodist Church. Fort Canning Road, Singapore

[298]
WESLEY METHODIST CHURCH, FORT CANNING
ROAD, SINGAPORE. (C 1910)

Back: Divided
Publisher: M.J., Penang

"The Bethesda", Singapore.

[299]
"THE BETHESDA", SINGAPORE.

Back: Divided
Publisher: Koh & Co., Singapore

A church along Bras Basah Road, the Bethesda
was demolished in the postwar years.

Wesley Church   Wesley Parsonage

Singapore

[300]
Untitled [A postcard with two views].
(c 1920)

Back: Divided
Publisher: Methodist Publishing House, Singapore

A postcard with two views: Wesley Church and
Wesley Parsonage.

[301]
Untitled [St. Joseph's Institution and the
Cathedral of the Good Shepherd]. (c 1890)
Back: Undivided

[302]
SINGAPORE. BRAS BASAH RD. WITH ST. JOSEPH'S SCHOOL. (1912)

Cancellation: 1912
Back: Divided
Series and/or No.: 254
Publisher: Max H. Hilckes, Singapore

[303]
ST. JOSEPH INSTITUTION, SINGAPORE. (1939)

Cancellation: 1939
Back: Divided

This postcard possesses a serrated left edge (it was torn from a postcard booklet).

Church of Good Shepherd, Singapore,

Cathedral of the "Good Shepherd", Singapore.

[304]

CHURCH OF GOOD SHEPHERD, SINGAPORE. (C 1910)

Back: Divided
Series and/or No.: 75
Publisher: Russian

A scene of the Church of the Good Shepherd and its towering spire.

[305]

CATHEDRAL OF THE "GOOD SHEPHERD", SINGAPORE. (C 1910)

Back: Divided
Series and/or No.:
Publisher: German

As viewed from the field along Queen Street, this is a scene of the Cathedral of the Good Shepherd.

[306]
THE CHURCH OF THE GOOD SHEPHERD,
SINGAPORE. (1924)

Cancellation: 1924
Back: Divided
Series and/or No.: H233
Publisher: Japanese

H 233   The Church of the good shepherd, Singapore.

Singapore
Caledonian Hotel.

[307]
SINGAPORE/CALEDONIAN HOTEL. (C 1910)

Back: Divided

The Caledonian Hotel at Bras Basah Road was later converted into the Japanese Commercial Museum while the Student House occupied the second floor[50].

AERIAL VIEW OF SINGAPORE

D 19

[308]
AERIAL VIEW OF SINGAPORE. (C 1940)

Back: Undivided

An aerial view of the Raffles museum and its surroundings; in front of the museum in the foreground was the YMCA building.

The Ladies'
Lawn Tennis Club
SINGAPORE

[309]
THE LADIES LAWN TENNIS CLUB SINGAPORE. (1908)

Cancellation: 1908
Back: Divided

The Ladies Lawn Tennis Club at the playing field along Bras Basah Road opposite the Cathay Cinema. This was its second club house[9]; the earlier one was at Penang Lane[57].

AERIAL VIEW FROM BRAS BASAH ROAD-S'PORE.

[310]
**AERIAL VIEW FROM BRAS BASAH ROAD –
S'PORE. (C 1940)**

Back: Divided

Presenting an aerial view of Bras Basah Road
from the Cathay Building, the tennis courts in the
playing field and the roof of the Ladies Lawn
Tennis Club (YWCA) are visible in the foreground.

D 41

AERIAL VIEW OF SINGAPORE

[311]
AERIAL VIEW OF SINGAPORE. (C 1940)

Series and/or No.: D 41
Back: Divided

A photographic postcard with an aerial view of
Selegie Road at its junction with Princep Street,
taken from Cathay Building. The building with a
large courtyard of parked vehicles was the
Registry of Vehicles.

Bras Basah Road, Singapore

[312]
BRAS BASAH ROAD, SINGAPORE. (1925)

Cancellation: 1925
Back: Divided
Series and/or No.: S.S. No. 14
Publisher: K.P. Hock, Singapore

Bras Basah Road at its junction with Dhoby Ghaut being occupied by the Lois Molteni Confectionery; it was very popular judging by the number of rickshaws, horse carriages and cars outside it.

CATHAY BUILDING, SINGAPORE.

[313]
CATHAY BUILDING, SINGAPORE. (C 1940)

Cancellation: 1953
Back: Divided

The Cathay Building was the first skyscraper to be built in Singapore in 1939.

Methodist Girls' School, Singapore.

[314]
METHODIST GIRLS' SCHOOL, SINGAPORE.
(C 1910)

Back: Divided
Publisher: Methodist Publishing House, Singapore

A view of Methodist Girls' School at Short Street, near Selegie Road.

Sophia Road, Singapore.

[315]
SOPHIA ROAD, SINGAPORE. (1911)

Cancellation: 1911
Back: Divided

The road was named after either Lady Sophia (Sir Stamford Raffles' second wife) or Mary Sophia Anne (daughter of Captain Flint, who was Sir Stamford's brother-in-law)[32].

ORCHARD and TANGLIN AREA

The Orchard Road Railway Bridge near Emerald Hill around 1920.
(*See* [319])

The Orchard Road Market (c 1900) with its striking red-brick facade and the Tan Kim Seng Fountain in front.
(*See* [325])

Orchard Road

Orchard Road was so named after the vast number of nutmeg plantations during its early days. "The hills around Orchard Road all the way to Tanglin were once covered with nutmeg trees… the hills have ever since resounded to the music of names given by the planters and land owners…"[30]

In the late 1800s and early 1900s[30], many churches as well as the rich started moving from the congested town area to the pleasant countryside that was Orchard Road then.

Photos [316-321] (*left, top*) show the Orchard Road area from 1890 to 1930. The Orchard Road market was built in 1894[29]; the land was originally part of the estate of William Cuppage (the Superintendent of the Police and Assistant Resident in 1846), and was bought by his son-in-law Edwin Koek in the 1860s. The fountain was removed from its original location at Telok Ayer Market around 1902.[5] Orchard Market is shown in [322; 323]; a vacant plot of land between the market and Orchard Road used by vendors since 1896; it was referred to as being "Koek's Bazaar" [323]. The brick façade was added later around 1905 [324; 325 (*left, middle*)]. The market was demolished in the 1970s to make way for the construction of the Orchard Point building.

Oldham Hall and St. Mary's Home

Oldham Hall, one of Singapore's first Boarding School for Boys [326], was located at 188 Orchard Road[34], the corner between Orchard Road and Oldham Lane[59] (adjacent to MacDonald House). William Fritzjames and his wife Marie had come to Singapore in 1885 to establish a Methodist Mission. They established the Anglo-Chinese School on Amoy Street; it was a school by day and a boarding house by night. In 1888, the boarders were relocated to a separate boarding house at Oldham Lane known as Bellevue. In 1902, the boarding house was renamed "Oldham Hall" in honour of Bishop Oldham, a Methodist Missionary. In 1926, Oldham Hall was moved to Barker Road. Since then, it has been rebuilt twice, in 1985 and 2001.[59]

St. Mary's Home [327] (which was located at Tank Road[34], now located at 207 Clemenceau Avenue) was "a home for resident pupils attending the day schools in Singapore. It was also an orphanage attached to the Home for Children. Fees from $20 per month included Board, Dhoby and School Fees."[34] Originally the house of Tan Yeok Nee (1827–1902), a Teochew towkay engaged in the pepper and gambier trade, it was acquired for use by the Tank Road Station master at the turn of the century when the Singapore-Johore Railway was being built. A decade later, the government had granted Tan's house to the Anglican Church, and the St. Mary's House and School for Eurasian Girls was established in 1912.[53] In 1938, the Salvation Army established their headquarters in Tan's House. It was gazetted as a national monument in 1974. Today, it is being used as the Asian campus for the University of Chicago Graduate School of Business.[53]

The YMCA of Singapore and the Presbyterian Church

The YMCA (Young Men's Christian Association) of Singapore stood at the junction of Fort Canning Road and Orchard Road from 1909 to 1981 [328]. It was first established in 1903 at Armenian Street by R.D. Pringle. Six years later, in recognition of its importance and usefulness, the government granted the YMCA a plot of land on Orchard Road. The foundation stone of the YMCA Building was first laid in 1909 by its patron, Sir

John Anderson (Governor, Straits Settlements, 1904–1911). He was to also oversee its official opening in 1911 [329 (*right, top*)]. In 1982, the building was demolished and a new nine-storey YMCA building was built on the site; it was officially opened in 1984 by E.W. Barker (Minister for Law, 1964–1988).[60]

The Presbyterian Church was located on Orchard Road [330; 331] and its origin can be traced back to the London Missionary Society (LMS) and the Presbyterian Church (England) Mission in South China. In 1839, LMS sent Benjamin Keasberry to work in Singapore where he established the Prinsep Street Presbyterian Church. In 1856, the Orchard Road Presbyterian Church was established to cater to its Scottish residents,[61] and its foundation stone was laid by Colonel Archibald Anson (Acting Governor, Straits Settlements, 1877).[4] In 1901, the Synod of the Nanyang Chinese Christian Presbyterian Church was formed; in 1971, the Orchard Road Presbyterian Church joined the Synod[61] and it has flourished till today.

The Government House (Istana)

In 1867, the Straits Settlements with Singapore as its capital, ceased to be a dependency of British India and was made a Crown Colony. Its first Colonial Governor, Sir Harry Ord (Governor, Straits Settlements, 1867–1873), commissioned the building of a Government House (now known as the Istana) [334-337] (*right, middle*) on land purchased from C.R. Princep's nutmeg estate. Convict labour was used to build this mansion, which was completed in 1869. One of its first guests was Admiral Sir Henry Keppel, who described it as "a palace". Unfortunately, the last Colonial Governor to stay there, Sir Shenton Thomas (Governor, Straits Settlements, 1934–1942; 1945–1946) and his wife, became prisoners-of-war during the Japanese Occupation.[30]

When Singapore attained self-rule in 1859, Yusof Ishak was appointed Singapore's first local head of state

(the Yang di-Pertuan Negara) and took up office at Government House. Today, the Istana is the official residence of the President of Singapore; the grounds are open to the public on certain holidays such as National Day. It is also mostly used for state functions and ceremonial purposes.[53]

The Istana underwent its first major renovation from 1996 to 1998.[62] Today it is a shining symbol of Singapore's historical and architectural legacy. The Istana garden occupies an area of 18,200 square metres with numerous shrubs, ornamental trees and fruit trees. Numerous species of birds and other fauna have also been observed and it also has a 9-hole golf course.[62]

Teutonia Club/Goodwood Park Hotel

The Teutonia (or German Club) was constructed in 1856. The first clubhouse (Blanche House) was built in 1862 in the vicinity of the new Teutonia Club (the old and new Teutonia Club [338]). The new Teutonia Club was located at Scotts Road [339-341], and was officially opened by Sir Frank Swettenham (Acting Governor, Straits Settlements, 1899–1901) in 1900.[9] It looked like a fairytale castle as it was fashioned after the castles on the Rhine.[30] The distinctive features of the building are in the South German Vernacular, exemplified here in the large semicircular gable ends, the surface ornamental relief and the enchanting tower with its pointed tiled roof.[30]

"The Teutonia Club held classical music concerts and snatches of Mozart or Beethoven were often heard by passerbys in that part of Scotts Road."[30]

During the First World War in 1914, the Teutonia Club was declared an enemy property, and it was converted into an electric power house for the next eight years. In 1929, the building was bought by the three Mennaseh brothers and they renamed it "Goodwood Hall" after the English home of the Duke of Richmond and Gordon.[30] It was to be reopened as a venue for concerts, dances, film shows and receptions. In later

YMCA building, Orchard Road, around 1940.
(*See* [329])

The full facade of the Government House (The Istana) around 1900.
(*See* [335])

The Teutonia Club around 1910.
(*See* [341])

The Singapore Botanic Gardens around 1900.
(*See* [353])

years, it was renamed again into what is known today as Goodwood Park Hotel [341 (*left, top*)].[30]

In 1963, Tan Sri Khoo Teck Puat, who was once known to be Singapore's richest man, bought the building from Mrs Elsie Mennaseh (who had inherited the hotel from the Mennaseh brothers); he rebuilt the historical tower and added new wings.[9,30] The Goodwood Park Hotel has since flourished and today, it is among Singapore's leading hotels.

Tanglin and Tanglin Barracks

The names of Tanglin and its namesake road are derived from the house of lawyer William Napier, who lived within its vicinity. Built in 1854, Napier's house was first called *tang leng* after the Chinese name *twa tang leng*, which means "great east hill peaks"; it was perhaps a reference to the numerous hills in that area.[32]

Where the Orchard Road stretch ends, the Tanglin District begins. In this area, two facilities were developed which survive to this day, namely the Tanglin Barracks (Military Barracks) [342-346] and the Botanic Gardens. In 1860, the Government purchased land at Tanglin for the construction of new barracks for European troops posted to Singapore. A big area including the nutmeg estate of W.E. Willans (Mount Harriet) was purchased for this purpose.[32]

The first occupants of the newly built Tanglin Barracks duly arrived in 1872. The Sherwood Foresters, a British Regiment, was stationed in Tanglin Barracks between December 1904 to December 1906[15] [347-349]; these ppcs were the earliest cards to have Divided-Backs and they were unusual as the date 1905 was printed on the cards (dates printed by publishers on ppcs are rare). Furthermore, these ppcs had embossed margins.

Singapore Botanic Gardens

The Singapore Botanic Gardens (SBC) [350-357] (*left, middle*) was created in 1859, after the Agri-Horticultural Society had been granted 32 hectares of land in Tanglin by the government, which had obtained it from Hoo Ah Kay (also known Whampoa), an early successful businessman famous for his beautiful garden, in exchange for land at Boat Quay. The SBC's first Superintendent and Landscape Designer, Lawrence Niven, was highly capable and the layout of the SBC today is largely based upon his designs. In 1874, the government took over the management of the Gardens.

However, each successive Director improved the Gardens in his own way; even during the Japanese Occupation (1942–1945), the Japanese Directors (Professors Tanakadate and Kwan Koriba) appreciated and kept the SBC intact. Today, the Singapore Botanic Gardens is a treasure trove for horticulturalists, botanists and nature lovers. Spread over 54 hectares, the SBC boasts several lakes, a topiary, a Japanese garden, and several colonial buildings, as well as an excellent orchid garden and 4.4 hectares of primary jungle.[9]

Singapore had another botanic garden – the Alkaff Gardens [358; 359]. Built in the 1929; it stretched from MacPherson Road to Serangoon Road. The Alkaff Gardens was closed and sold in 1949, and the land was developed in the 1960s into what is now known as the Sennett Estate.[9]

New Tyersall

Adjacent to the Singapore Botanic Gardens was New Tyersall, the Singapore residence of the Sultan of Johore. The original house, Tyersall, had been built by William Napier on 67 acres of land in 1854.[58] Later purchased by Sultan Abu Bakar of Johore (1831– 1895), Napier's house was demolished to make way for a new palace; this palace was called New Tyersall and it was completed in 1892 [360; 361]. The building was designed in Corinthian style with a red tiled roof and a tower nearly 70 feet high. Unfortunately, the Palace was destroyed by fire on 10 September 1905; it was never rebuilt.[58]

Orchard Road Singapore

[316]
ORCHARD ROAD SINGAPORE. (C 1890)

Back: Divided
Publisher: Russian

The area is surrounded by nutmeg trees; a sole bullock-cart stands in the middle of the road.

Singapore. Orchard Road.

[317]
SINGAPORE. ORCHARD ROAD. (C 1900)

Cancellation: 1904
Back: Undivided

The road has few users (coolies, bullock-carts and a horse) and is surrounded by lush greeneries.

Orchard Road, Singapore.

[318]
ORCHARD ROAD, SINGAPORE. (1911)

Cancellation: 1911
Back: Divided
Publisher: Kong Hing Chiong & Co., North Bridge Road, Singapore

The Presbyterian Church can be seen on the left; the road had railings on the right and the road traffic consisted of rickshaws.

Orchard Road, Singapore

[319]
ORCHARD ROAD SINGAPORE. (C 1913)

Back: Divided
Series and/or No.: Singapore No. 1016
Publisher: The Continental Stamp Company, Singapore

This view looks northwards and shows the Orchard Road Railway Bridge near Emerald Hill. From 1903 to 1932, trains ran from Tank Road Railway Station across this bridge to the Woodlands Jetty.

[320]
ORCHARD ROAD SINGAPORE. (C 1928)

Cancellation: 1928
Back: Divided

A photographic postcard of the Amber Mansions (demolished c 1990s) and the Keller piano shop opposite it.

[321]
ORCHARD ROAD, SINGAPORE. (C 1930)

Back: Divided
Publisher: M.W.P., Singapore

A sepia-toned postcard that provides an overview of Orchard Road; the Tan Kim Seng Fountain can be seen on the left at its junction with Koek Road.

[322]
SINGAPORE. ORCHARD ROAD MARKET. (C 1900)

Cancellation: 1914
Back: Divided
Publisher: Koh & Co., Singapore

[323]
MARKET SCENE, SINGAPORE. (C 1900)

Back: Divided

Depicts the market scene in Orchard Road and of "Koek's Bazaar". The vacant space between it and Orchard Road was used by vendors since 1896[5].

A market at Orchard Road, Singapore.

[324]
A MARKET AT ORCHARD ROAD, SINGAPORE. (C 1905)

Cancellation: 1907
Back: Divided

A sepia-toned postcard showing the market at the junction of Orchard Road and Koek Road.

(26) Orchard Road Market, Singapore.

[325]
ORCHARD ROAD MARKET, SINGAPORE. (C 1910)

Back: Divided
Publisher: Russian

The Orchard Road Market with its striking red-brick facade and the Tan Kim Seng Fountain in front.

"Oldham Hall", a Boarding School for Boys, Singapore.

[326]
"OLDHAM HALL" A BOARDING SCHOOL FOR
BOYS, SINGAPORE. (C 1900)

Back: Divided
Publisher: Methodist Publishing House, Singapore

It stood at the corner of Orchard Road and
Oldham Lane.

Singapore - St. Mary's Home

[327]
SINGAPORE. ST. MARY'S HOME. (C 1920)

Back: Divided
Publisher: Koh & Co., Singapore

St. Mary's Home in the House of Towkay Tan
Yeok Nee.

Y. M. C. A. Building, Singapore

[328]
Y.M.C.A. BUILDING, SINGAPORE. (C 1915)

Back: Divided
Publisher: Methodist Publishing House, Singapore

A close-up view of the YMCA.

M 21. Y.M.C.A. BLDG: S'PORE

[329]
Y.M.C.A. BLDG, S'PORE. (C 1940)

Back: Divided
Series and/or No.: M 21

Singapore. Presbyterian Church.

[330]
SINGAPORE. PRESBYTERIAN CHURCH. (C 1900)

Cancellation: 1911
Back: Divided
Publisher: Wilson & Co., Hotel de l'Europe & Orchard Road, Singapore

The Presbyterian Church at Orchard Road and adjacent to the YMCA was built in 1877; it has continued to function till this day.

Presbyterian Church, Singapore.

[331]
PRESBYTERIAN CHURCH, SINGAPORE. (C 1920)

Back: Divided
Publisher: German

[332]
SINGAPORE, SCOTCH AND STEVENS ROAD.
(C 1900)

Back: Divided
Series and/or No.: 255
Photographer: Max H. Hilckes, Singapore

Shows Stevens Road on the postcard's left hand side and Scotts (misspelt as "Scotch" in the postcard) Road on its right, as looking from Orchard Road around 1900.

[333]
SINGAPORE, STREET SCENE. (C 1910)

Back: Divided
Publisher: Wilson & Co., Hotel de l'Europe & Orchard Road, Singapore

This postcard shows a rickshaw, a bullock-cart and a fruit seller at the entrance of the Teutonia club.

[334]
ENTRANCE TO THE GOVERNMENT HOUSE, SINGAPORE. (C 1900)

Cancellation: 1907
Back: Divided
Publisher: Russian

[335]
SINGAPORE, GOVERNMENT HOUSE. (C 1900)

Cancellation: 1906
Back: Undivided

The full façade of the Government House.

Singapore. Government House.

72

[336]
SINGAPORE. GOVERNMENT HOUSE. (C 1900)

Back: Undivided

The Government House with its large manicured ground and numerous flora and fauna.

GOVERNMENT GARDEN, SINGAPORE

[337]
GOVERNMENT GARDEN, SINGAPORE. (C 1940)

Back: Divided

The garden of the Government House; the postcard has a left serrated edge (it was torn from a postcard booklet).

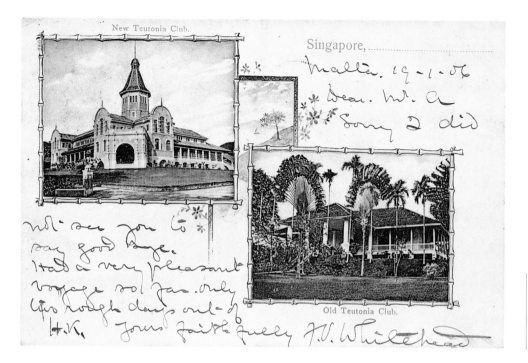

[338]

Untitled [The old and new Teutonia Club].

Cancellation: 1906
Back: Undivided
Series and/or No.: 78032

The old Club was built in 1886 and the new Club was built in 1900.

[339]

Teutonia Club, Singapore. (c 1900)

Cancellation: 1902
Back: Undivided
Publisher: Stengel & Co., Dresden u. Berlin

A rare multiview postcard showing seven views of the Teutonia Club; the exterior and interior of the club are depicted.

Teutonic Club, Singapore.

[340]
TEUTONIA CLUB, SINGAPORE. (1909)

Cancellation: 1909
Back: Divided
Publisher: German

Singapore, Teutonia Club.

[341]
SINGAPORE, TEUTONIA CLUB. (C 1910)

Back: Divided
Series and/or No.: 657

The Teutonia Club is seen proudly flying the German flag from the top of its tower.

TANGLIN BARRACKS, SINGAPORE

[342]
TANGLIN BARRACKS, SINGAPORE. (C 1900)
Back: Divided
Series and/or No.: 2518-a
Publisher: Gale & Polden, Ltd, Aldershot

TANGLIN BARRACKS, SINGAPORE

[343]
TANGLIN BARRACKS, SINGAPORE. (C 1900)
Back: Divided
Series and/or No.: 2518-a
Publisher: Gale & Polden, Ltd, Aldershot

Tanglin Barracks - Singapore

[344]
TANGLIN BARRACKS – SINGAPORE. (C 1900)

Back: Divided
Series and/or No.: Singapore No. 41
Publisher: The Continental Stamp Company, Singapore

Overlooking Napier and Holland Roads, and the Botanic Gardens. This site is now the present location of the Ministry of Foreign Affairs.

Hospital – Tanglin Barracks.

[345]
HOSPITAL – TANGLIN BARRACKS.

Back: Divided
Publisher: G.R. Lambert & Co., Singapore

The hospital in Tanglin Barracks set amidst luscious greenery.

[346]
THE GOLF LINKS – TANGLIN BARACKS. (c 1900)
Back: Divided
Publisher: G.R. Lambert & Co., Singapore

[347]
OFFICERS MESS PLATE – I. SHERWOOD
FORESTERS. – 1905.
Back: Divided
Series and/or No.: XLV Series C
Publisher: G.R. Lambert & Co., Singapore

[348]
W.Os Staff Sergeants and Sergeants –I. Sherwood Foresters – 1905.

Back: Divided
Series and/or No.: XLV Series A
Publisher: G.R. Lambert & Co., Singapore

[349]
Staff – I. Sherwood Foresters – 1905.

Back: Divided
Series and/or No.: XLV Series B
Publisher: G.R. Lambert & Co., Singapore

[350]
ESTRANCE OF SINGAPORE GARDEN. (C 1900)

Back: Divided
Publisher: Russian

Entrance to the Botanic Gardens from Cluny Road; note the bright red flowers of the flame-of-the-forest trees.

[351]
BOTANICAL GARDEN. SINGAPORE. (C 1930)

Cancellation: 1929
Back: Divided

Botanic Gardens from the corner of Holland and Cluny Roads.

Para Rubber Tree, Singapore

[352]
PARA RUBBER TREE, SINGAPORE. (C 1900)

Back: Divided
Publisher: Russian

The placard besides the tree reads "Para Rubber/Herea/Brazileensis/Planted 1879". This was the first rubber tree to be planted in the Botanic Gardens.

Botanical Garden, Singapore

[353]
BOTANIC GARDEN, SINGAPORE. (C 1900)

Back: Divided
Series and/or No.: Singapore No. 1031
Publisher: The Continental Stamp Company, Singapore

Two European gentlemen dressed in white jackets and hats sitting on a bench besides the lake.

Singapore. Bot. Garden, Victoria Regia.

[354]
SINGAPORE. BOT. GARDEN, VICTORIA REGIA.
(1902)

Cancellation: 1902
Back: Undivided

This picture postcard shows the giant Victoria lily in the lake. Postcards with Queen Victoria stamps on the picture side are uncommon.

The Water Lilies, Botanical Gardens, Singapore.

[355]
THE WATER LILIES, BOTANICAL GARDENS,
SINGAPORE. (1912)

Back: Divided
Publisher: Koh & Co., Singapore

Depicts lotus plants growing in a pond in the Botanic Gardens.

No. 122 Orchid House, Bot. Gardens.

[356]
ORCHID HOUSE, BOT. GARDENS. (C 1930)

Back: Divided
Series and/or No.: 122
Publisher: German

The techniques of orchid hybridisation was developed by Prof. Eric Holtum when he was Director of the Gardens from 1925 to 1949.

SINGAPORE
The Herbarium, Botanical Garden

[357]
SINGAPORE. THE HERBARIUM, BOTANICAL GARDEN. (C 1930)

Back: Divided
Publisher: G.R. Lambert & Co., Singapore

5 "The Lake" in Alkaff Garden in Japaness design.

[358]
"THE LAKE" IN ALKAFF GARDEN IN JAPANESE
DESIGN. (1935)

Back: Divided
Series and/or No.: 5

Located in Sennett Estate from 1929–1949, the
Alkaff Garden was Singapore's "second botanic
gardens". Set in a Japanese design, the Lake's
bridges and pavilions are also Japanese-inspired
designs.

Alkaff Garden, Singapore.

[359]
ALKAFF GARDEN, SINGAPORE. (C 1940)

Back: Divided

The land which Alkaff Garden stood on was
developed into the Sennett Estate in the 1960s.
Today, all that remains of the Alkaff's name is
the old Alkaff Mosque in the vicinity.

SINGAPORE, "Tyersall" Residence Sultan of Johore

[360]
SINGAPORE. "TYERSALL" RESIDENCE SULTAN OF
JOHORE. (C 1900)

Back: Divided
Series and/or No.: 196
Publisher: Max H. Hilckes, Singapore

New Tyersall, palace of the Sultan of Johore in
Singapore stood adjacent to the Singapore
Botanic Gardens around 1900. It stood on 67
acres of garden.

The Sultan's Residential Palace, Singapore

[361]
THE SULTAN'S RESIDENTIAL PALACE,
SINGAPORE.

Back: Divided
Series and/or No.: 39
Publisher: Koh & Co., Singapore

New Tyersall was built in 1892 and destroyed by
fire in 1905.

SUBURBAN, RURAL and COASTAL AREAS

Rochor canal at around 1920; a herd of buffalos and its Indian keeper are in the river.
(*See* [365])

Lavender Street as depicted around the early 1900s.
(*See* [367])

Serangoon Road and Vicinity

The Serangoon Road area is often referred to as "Little India", the locus of Singapore Indian retailing, culture and festivities. The origin of the name "Serangoon" is uncertain; it could have been derived from the *burong ranggong*, a marsh bird commonly found in the swamps of the Serangoon River (formerly the Rangon River), or it could have originated from the Malay words *diserang dengan gong* (to attack with gongs or drums). In the past, people on the way to Johore travelled through the Serangoon area first, and they had to use gongs to frighten off wild animals.[32]

The main occupants of the area were Indian migrants from India who had since 1826, come to Singapore to work on brick kilns and cattle industries. Around 1900, Serangoon Road was still very much a largely deserted country road[63] [362; 363].

Like Serangoon, Rochor is also part of old colonial Singapore. There are two versions concerning the origins of the name Rochor.[32] One has it that it was derived from the Chinese words *Wu Zhu*, which alluded to the Five Ancestors who sailed up the Rochor Canal and settled on its banks. Another interpretation suggests that "Rochor" was derived from the Malay word *Rochoh* (meaning to make marks with a pointed stick).[32]

In 1819, the Rochor River (Canal) was navigable for some distance inland and many Orang Lauts and Malays settled on its bank [364]. Indians also came from Serangoon to settle down as their buffalos required plenty of water [365 (*left, top*)]. Many plantations (gambier, pepper, coffee and sugar) were also found in early Rochor.[64]

Constructed in the 1880s, the Jalan Besar area was originally just a plot of swampy land. However, its name indicates it was either a big or wide road [366; 369]. It is also known to the Hokkiens as *kam kong ka poh tu long*, a reference to the abattoir [368] in the vicinity. This slaughter house and another at Pulau Saigon were set up in 1892 to control unlicensed and unregistered slaughter premises.[4]

Lavender Street [367 (*left, middle*)] connects the Rochor Bridge to Serangoon; it was officially named in 1858. At that time, the area was covered by Chinese vegetable farms; the smell was unbearable due to the use of night soil as fertiliser. Because of this, its residents referred sarcastically to the area as Lavender Street.[32]

The longest (25 km) road in Singapore, the Bukit Timah Road [370; 371] runs from the north (Serangoon) to the south (Woodlands) of the island. It literally means "tin bearing hill" in Malay although the origin of its name remains uncertain.[32] Other landmarks in the area included the Singapore Electric Tramway Power Station, the water treatment reservoir and the Race Course.

Bidadari Cemetery [372; 373] is sandwiched between Upper Serangoon Road and Sennett Estate. The word *bidadari* means "fairy"; the cemetery took its name from the beautiful wife of the Maharajah Abu Bakar of Johore, who had a house here.[32] The cemetery was opened on 15 December 1907 and it had Protestant and Catholic sections complete with its own chapel.[65] The European victims of the Sepoy (Indian) Mutiny in 1915 were also buried there.[29] Today, the graves in Bidadari Cemetery are being exhumed, and soon another historic landscape will be erased.

The Singapore Sporting Club was founded in 1843; the name was changed to the Singapore Turf Club in 1924 [375 (*right, top*)]. It was situated at Farrer Park [374; 376] from 1843 to 1935 before shifting to a larger plot of land (250 acres) in Bukit Timah [377; 378], in response to its rapidly increasing number of members.[9]

The Tan Tock Seng Hospital [379] in Moulmein Road was named after Tan Tock Seng (1798–1850), a Singaporean merchant and philanthropist. Tan Tock Seng had in 1844 donated $7,000 to build a hospital for "the sick of all nations"[33] (Pauper's Hospital) on Pearl's Hill and it was so named after him.

The foundation stone of the first Tan Tock Seng Hospital was laid on 25 May 1844 at Pearl's Hill. Since then, the hospital has moved twice: Serangoon Road (1858–1908) and Moulmein Road (1909–present).[32] His son (Tan Kim Ching) and widow (Lee Seo Neo) made further donations to the hospital. Further benefactors of the hospital include Syed Ali bin Mohamed Junied (who in 1857 donated 5 acres of land with houses) and Towkay Loke Yew (he donated $50,000 in 1909).[33]

During the Japanese Occupation (1942–1945), the Tan Tock Seng Hospital remained the main hospital for civilians and it was briefly renamed *Hakuai Byoin* (Universal Love Hospital) by the Japanese. Today, Tan Tock Seng Hospital has progressed from being a pauper's hospital to an ultra modern restructured general hospital.

The Reservoirs

Singapore's survival depended largely on its attractiveness to trading vessels; it was highly important that vessels be induced to touch at the port for fresh water.[29] In 1852, a report was made by J.T. Thomson, proposing a scheme for the supply of water to town from the headwaters of the "Singapore Creek".

The impounding reservoir at Thomson Road [380; 381] remained Singapore's only source of water till 1900;

it was enlarged in 1891 and 1904.[29] In 1900, the Kallang River Reservoir [382] was constructed and it was officially opened on 26 March 1912 [383 (*right, middle*)]. Each impounding reservoir required supplementary service reservoirs to allow the water to reach the houses by gravitation and the first service reservoir was built at Mount Emily [384] around 1878. Other supplementary service reservoirs [385] were built later at Pearl's Hill and Government Hill (Fort Canning).

Thomson Road Reservoir was renamed MacRitchie Reservoir in the early 1920s after James MacRitchie, the Municipal Engineer who was largely responsible for waterworks between 1883 and 1895.[32] In 1922, Kallang River Reservoir was renamed Peirce Reservoir after Robert Peirce, the Municipal Engineer from 1901 to 1916, who had constructed the reservoir. In 1975, a major water supply project to develop new water resources was undertaken to support Singapore's rapid housing and industrialisation programmes, and a dam was constructed at the upper reaches of the Peirce Reservoir, and this formed the Upper Peirce and Lower Peirce Reservoirs.[66]

Geylang and Kallang

The place Geylang [386] and the name Geylang Serai are found early on in Singapore's history. Although the origin of "Geylang" remains uncertain, it could have been derived from the Malay word *kilang* (meaning mill) as there were coconut plantations and mills located at Geylang Road. Another theory has it that it was named after the fierce *orang gallangs* (sea gypsies) [388] that lived along the coasts and rivers of Singapore.[32]

Geylang Serai refers to the areas around Geylang where the cultivation of *serai* (lemongrass or citronella) was common in early Singapore. Today Geylang Serai is considered the traditional cultural heartland of the Malays[32] and it is commonly known as the "Malay Emporium of Singapore".[67]

The race course of the Singapore Turf Club at Farrer Park in 1924.
(*See* [375])

The opening ceremony of the Kallang River Reservoir in 1912.
(*See* [383])

Two European men with white jackets and hats walking along the Tanjong Rhu Slipway, around 1910.
(*See* [391])

A tranquil picture of coconut trees by the seaside at Tanjong Katong around 1910.
(*See* [394])

Kallang is an old Malay reference to the Orang Lauts (sea gypsies), otherwise called *orang biduanda kallang*, who lived along the Kallang and Singapore rivers. Another explanation is that it had been derived from the Malay word *galang* (to put a boat on wooden rollers), an apt term as the Kallang area straddles both sides of the Kallang River.[32] Tanjong Rhu was formerly known as Sandy Point. *Tanjong* in Malay means peninsula and the word *rhu* is derived from *pokok rhu* (casuarinas tree) that grew along the beach; thus Tanjong Rhu is an area of land that protrudes into the sea lined by casuarinas trees.

In Tanjong Rhu [389], the Tanjong Rhu Slipway [390; 391 (*left, top*)] has been in existence since the 1880s when William and Campbell Heard and Co. erected a ship slipway at Tanjong Rhu. The Singapore Slipway was finally established in 1887 and the two largest ship repair yards in Singapore then, Tanjong Pagar Dock Co. and the New Harbour Dock Co. owned shares in the company.

The Singapore Swimming Club (SSC) [392] is situated at 45 Tanjong Rhu; it was founded in 1893. In 1931, a swimming pool and club house were built, and the Club catered only to Europeans till 1963.[68] In the 1900s, the waters off Tanjong Rhu were shark-infested; hence the swimming area in front of the club was enclosed with steel fences [393]. The SSC is now located well inland following the Government's East Coast reclamation scheme in the 1970s.[9]

Katong and Tanjong Katong

Katong is the name of an extinct species of sea turtle; it also means the rippling effect of a sea mirage when looking at a shore line.[32]

Known to be an enclave of Eurasians in the early 1900s, the history of Katong is linked to the development of cotton and coconut plantations. William Farquhar, the first Resident of Singapore, started a coconut estate in the district. Pioneer estate owners included Thomas

Dunman, Thomas Crane, Jose d'Almeida, John Armstrong, Hoo Ah Kay and the Little family.[32]

Tanjong Katong, an early landmark in Singapore, is also the Malay name for "turtle point". An idyllic picture of coconut trees swaying by the seaside, Tanjong Katong was up to the 20th century, the holiday resort area for rich town dwellers [394-396][32] (*left, middle*). The Catholic Christian Brothers also had a bungalow [399] on the site of the present St. Patrick's School in Marine Parade Road, near Katong. It was built around 1898 and demolished in 1929 to make way for St. Patrick's School.[69]

The Sea View Hotel [400-405] at Tanjong Katong was founded in the late 1890s. [400] shows the hotel with its tennis court amidst coconut trees by the seaside, while its obverse states that its proprietor was W. Percy Spiers. The hotel was finally sold to the Sarkies brothers in 1923[4] and it functioned till the 1960s before being demolished in the 1970s; on its site along Meyer Road were built modern bungalows.[9] The Sea View Hotel was also once used as a sanatorium.

Joo Chiat Road [397] and Siglap [398] are adjacent to Katong.

Rural and Coastal Areas

There are many ppcs of prewar Singapore showing rural and coastal scenes. [406] shows Thomson Road around 1900; it is in central Singapore. Known as Seletar Road up to the 1850s, the road was renamed after John Turnball Thomson, the Government Surveyor (1841–1853). The Chinese refer to Thomson Road as *chia chwi kang* or "fresh water stream" (a reference to the Kallang River that flows by it).[32] The Sembawang market [407] was located not far from Thomson Road.

Punggol (or Ponggol) and Bedok [408; 409] are another two coastal areas located at the northern and eastern tips of Singapore. Punggol means in Malay "hurling sticks at the branches of fruit trees to bring them down to the ground"[32], and it was a rural area of farm structures. It was also the stronghold of the Teochews and Catholics.[32] Bedok, however, is an early native place and it has been in existence since the time of Sir Stamford Raffles. The Malay word *bedoh* refers to a large drum that calls people to a mosque; the "h" in *bedoh* is pronounced as a "k", hence the word "Bedok".[32]

At the southern tip of Singapore is the coastal area of Pasir Panjang [410]. The Malay words *pasir panjang* literally mean "long sand". In the 1920 to 30s, many holiday bungalows were built in Pasir Panjang by wealthy Chinese. (e.g. Haw Par Villa [411])

Islands around Singapore

St. John's Island (Pulau Sakijang Bandera) [412 (*right, top*)] in Malay (*si kijang*) means "barking deer" when translated. However, the name St. John's is said to be an English mispronunciation of *si kijang* during Sir Stamford Raffles' first visit to the island.[32] The island was once used as an infectious diseases hospital following the cholera epidemic in Singapore in 1873[29]. It was also used as a drug rehabilitation centre and a place of exile for political dissidents.[53] Today, St. John is a popular weekend retreat; it is about 6.5 km south of Singapore and it is a 40-minute boat ride away from Singapore.

Pulau Blakang Mati (Sentosa) [413] is famous today as a resort and theme park island. It is set to be even more famous when an integrated resort (with a casino) is built on it in a few years' time. During the colonial era, the island was used by the British Military and a hospital named "HMS Sultan" was established on it during the 1950s. In 1967, it was taken over by the Singapore Navy but by the 1970s, it had been converted into a theme park island. Its original name of *Blakang Mati* in Malay means "dead back" or "behind the dead". How it got such an unpropitious name is uncertain[32] but its name was changed to Sentosa (Isle of peace and tranquility) in 1972.

Pulau Brani [414] when translated from Malay means "Island of the Brave". It is located south of Singapore near Keppel Harbour and is sandwiched between Singapore and Sentosa. It is also linked to Singapore via Brani Terminal Avenue. During the colonial era, Pulau Brani was used as a navy/military fort. It was redeveloped as a naval base in 1971, and in 1974, the Singapore Maritime Command Naval Base on Pulau Brani was officially opened. Today, Pulau Brani is an important naval base (Brani Base) and a busy port.[32]

Pulau Bukum [415] is an island situated south of Singapore. The island's name is thought to have originated from the Malay word *rangkek bukom*, a seashell which is wide at one end and tapers to a narrow point. It was also the shape of the island prior to human modifications.[32] The island is currently the site of oil refineries belonging to Shell, a petroleum company. Shell's association with the island dates back to 1891, when the company used the island for storing kerosene.[32]

Kusu Island (also spelt koosoo) [416] means Tortoise Island in Chinese; it is also known as "Peak Island" or *Pulau Tembakul* in Malay. The island is shaped like a turtle's back and legend has it that two fishermen (one Malay and the other, a Chinese) caught in a storm were saved by a turtle. Eternally grateful, both fishermen became sworn brothers and lived on the island harmoniously.[32] Every year during the 9th lunar month, thousands of Chinese come to the island to pray to the resident deity, whose spirit is said to infuse pilgrims with supernatural powers.[32] Located just 5.6 km south of Singapore, Kusu Island is also well loved for its blue lagoons, pristine beaches and tranquil settings.

The Raffles Lighthouse [417 (*right, middle*)] was built on Coney Island (also known as Pulau Satumu) in 1856. It is located 13 miles to the southwest of Singapore, and marks the Outer and South Channel round St. John's Island in the Singapore Roads.[18] It is today also well known for the many pristine diving sites around it.

St. John's Island around 1920.
(*See* [412])

The Raffles Lighthouse was built in 1856 on Coney Island.
(*See* [417])

(87)

Selangoon Road, Singapore

[362]

SELANGOON ROAD, SINGAPORE. (C 1900)

Back: Divided
Publisher: Russian

Serangoon was also spelt "Selangoon". A deserted country road with few rickshaws and pedestrians.

Singapore. Recreation Hotel. Serangoon Road.

[363]

SINGAPORE. RECREATION HOTEL. SERANGOON ROAD. (C 1900)

Cancellation: 1909
Back: Divided

The Recreation Hotel has since been demolished and its original location could be sited in the vicinity of the market in Upper Serangoon.

Malay village on the Rochor river, Singapore

[364]
MALAY VILLAGE ON THE ROCHOR RIVER,
SINGAPORE. (C 1910)

Back: Divided
Publisher: Japanese

Showing boats, people and houses (on stilts)
along the Rochor River.

Singapore Road and Rochor Road

[365]
SINGAPORE ROAD AND ROCHOR ROAD. (C 1920)

Back: Divided
Publisher: Russian

A herd of buffalos and its Indian keeper are in
the Rochor Canal.

Cotton Plants at Jalan Busar, Singapore.

20 €

[366]
COTTON PLANTS AT JALAN BESAR, SINGAPORE.
(C 1900)

Back: Divided

Cotton plants along Jalan Besar; at that time, Jalan Besar was renowned for cotton trees; a bullock-cart and cyclist are identifiable in the postcard.

(90)   Lavender Street, Singapore

[367]
LAVENDER STREET, SINGAPORE. (C 1900)

Cancellation: 1919
Back: Divided
Publisher: Russian

Depicts a lateritic road, with swampy vegetable farms in the background.

Slaughter House, Lalan Besar, Singapore.

[368]
SLAUGHTER HOUSE, LALAN BESAR, SINGAPORE.
(c 1910)

Back: Divided
Publisher: Russian

The Municipal Abattoir at Jalan Besar. It was built in 1891 and first used in 1894. The word "Jalan" is misspelt as "Lalan" in the postcard.

[369]
JALAN BESAR SINGAPORE. (c 1940)

Back: Divided

A photographic postcard showing the Ngung Hin Hotel and the Ngung Huat Restaurant along Jalan Besar. Note the building's beautiful plaster decorations and Peranakan tiles. The building is still standing today.

Bukit Timah Church, Singapore

[370]
BUKIT TIMAH CHURCH, SINGAPORE. (C 1900)

Back: Divided
Publisher: Kong Hing Chiong & Co., North Bridge Road, Singapore

The exact location of this church remains uncertain.

Singapore. Bukit Timah Bungalow.

[371]
SINGAPORE. BUKIT TIMAH BUNGALOW. (C 1900)

Back: Divided

An European stands outside his bungalow with several servants.

[372]
BIDADARI CEMETERY – SINGAPORE. (1910)

Cancellation: 1910
Back: Divided
Series and/or No.: 8
Publisher: The Continental Stamp Company, Singapore

The ornate gates at the entrance to Bidadari Christian Cemetery; the chapel can be seen behind the entrance gates.

[373]
BIDADARI CEMETERY – SINGAPORE. (C 1910)

Back: Divided
Series and/or No.: 36
Publisher: The Continental Stamp Company, Singapore

A view of the Bidadari Cemetery along Upper Serangoon Road showing the side view of the chapel.

Grand Stand Race Course, Singapore

[374]
GRAND STAND RACE COURSE, SINGAPORE.
(C 1900)

Back: Divided
Publisher: Russian

A view of the Grand Stand Race Course at Farrer Park.

Race Course - Singapore

[375]
RACE COURSE – SINGAPORE. (C 1920)

Back: Divided
Series and/or No.: 24
Publisher: The Continental Stamp Company, Singapore

Cryers at the Race Course, Singapore

[376]
CRYERS AT RACE COURSE, SINGAPORE. (C 1900)

Back: Divided
Publisher: M.J., Penang

Horse racing was popular in prewar Singapore and the crowd was multinational (Chinese with pigtails, Malays and Europeans in the postcard).

SINGAPORE RACE COURSE

[377]
SINGAPORE RACE COURSE. (C 1940)

Back: Divided

Depicts the grandstand of the new Singapore Race Course at Bukit Timah. It was packed on racing days and could accommodate more than 4,000 people.

[378]
RACE COURSE. SINGAPORE. (C 1940)
Back: Divided

The Singapore Race Course at Bukit Timah was packed on a race day.

[379]
WARDS OF TAN TOCK SENG'S HOSPITAL, SINGAPORE. (1921)
Cancellation: 1921
Back: Divided
Series and/or No.: 79

A photographic postcard showing the "open wards" (single storey building with large doors and windows to minimise cross infections) of Tan Tock Seng Hospital.

The Lake is Impounding Reservoir Thomson Road, Singapore.

[380]
THE LAKE IS IMPOUNDING RESERVOIR
THOMSON ROAD, SINGAPORE. (C 1900)

Back: Divided
Publisher: Japanese

Reservoir Singapore.

[381]
RESERVOIR SINGAPORE. (C 1920)

Cancellation: 1923
Back: Divided

Another view of the impounding reservoir at
Thomson Road.

Kalang River Reservoir.
The largest one in Singapore. Top water area 253 acres, depth 27 feet,
available Storage 211 days supply at the rate of 3 500 000 gallons per day

[382]
KALANG RIVER RESERVOIR. (C 1910)

Back: Divided
Series and/or No.: 16
Publisher: Koh & Co., Singapore

The Kallang River Reservoir was constructed in 1900 and was then the largest reservoir in Singapore.

Kalang River Reservoir — Opening of new Works 26th March 1912

[383]
KALANG RIVER RESERVOIR – OPENING OF NEW WORKS 26TH MARCH 1912.

Cancellation: 1916
Back: Divided
Series and/or No.: 17
Publisher: Koh & Co., Singapore

Depicts the opening ceremony of the Kallang River Reservoir.

Singapore. Waterworks Governement.

[384]
SINGAPORE. WATERWORKS GOVERNMENT.
(C 1890)

Back: Divided
Publisher: Max H. Hilckes, Singapore

Shows the Service Reservoir at Mount Emily, the Government House (Istana) can be seen in the postcard's background (top left).

Bukit Timah Reservoir, Singapore

[385]
BUKIT TIMAH RESERVOIR, SINGAPORE. (C 1913)

Cancellation: 1913
Back: Divided
Series and/or No.: 1009
Publisher: The Continental Stamp Company, Singapore

The filtration pumps at Bukit Timah Road; they are located opposite the Kandang Kerbau Women's and Children's Hospital; they are still standing.

Singapore. Suburban, Police Station.

[386]
SINGAPORE. SUBURBAN, POLICE STATION.
(1902)

Cancellation: 1902
Back: Undivided

This postcard shows the Geylang Police Station along a deserted Geylang Road. A policeman is standing outside the police station. This postcard has a Queen Victoria 1¢ stamp on the picture side, and this is rare.

(91)   Gus Works, Gelang Road, Singapore

[387]
GAS WORKS, GELANG ROAD, SINGAPORE.
(C 1910)

Back: Divided
Series and/or No.: 11
Publisher: Russian

The Gas Works at Geylang Road were also known as the Municipal Gas Works. The word "Geylang" is misspelt as "Gelang".

[388]
CAMPONG KALLANG. (1908)

Cancellation: 1908
Back: Divided
Publisher: G.R. Lambert & Co., Singapore

Depicts Malay houses on stilts, boats and Malay children by the side of the Kallang river.

[389]
TANJONG RHU SINGAPORE. (C 1930)

Back: Divided

A photographic postcard showing Malay huts on stilts, boats and factories (mills) with tall chimneys in the background.

Tanjong Rhu Slipway, Singapore.

[390]
TANJONG RHU SLIPWAY, SINGAPORE. (1908)

Cancellation: 1908
Back: Divided
Publisher: German

The Tanjong Rhu Slipway was in existence from the 1880s to the 1980s.

Tanjong Rhu Slipway, Singapore.

[391]
TANJONG RHU SLIPWAY, SINGAPORE. (C 1910)

Back: Divided
Publisher: German

Two European men with white jackets and hats walking besides a half-constructed ship.

[392]

SWIMMING CLUB SINGAPORE. (C 1940)

Back: Divided

A photographic postcard showing the Singapore Swimming Club; the swimming pool, diving stage and clubhouse are shown.

[393]

SWIMMING CLUB SINGAPORE. (C 1940)

Back: Divided

Showing the sea in front of the club enclosed by steel fencing (foreground) to keep out sharks.

Tanjong Katong, Singapore.

[394]
TANJONG KATONG, SINGAPORE. (C 1910)

Back: Divided
Series and/or No.: 1059
Publisher: The Continental Stamp Company, Singapore

This postcard depicts a tranquil picture of coconut trees swaying by the seaside at Tanjong Katong.

Singapore. Tanjong Katong Villa.

[395]
SINGAPORE. TANJONG KATONG VILLA. (C 1900)

Back: Divided

A rich man's villa in the style of an eclectic European bungalow.

[396]
SINGAPORE TANJONG KATONG. SEA SIDE. VILLA. (1916)

Cancellation: 1916
Back: Divided
Publisher: Japanese

The villa had two hexagonal cupolas; its garden gates were surmounted by a large pair of eagles with outstretched wings (commonly seen in Chinese residences).

233

[397]
JOO CHIAT ROAD SINGAPORE. (C 1930)

Back: Divided

A photographic postcard depicting Joo Chiat Road at around 1930; the road was beginning to become congested with motorcars and rickshaws.

[398]
SIGLAP (9TH MILESTONE) POLICE STATION,
SINGAPORE. (C 1930)

Back: Divided
Publisher: Koh & Co., Singapore

[399]
BROTHERS' BUNGALOW. SINGAPORE. (C 1913)

Cancellation: 1913
Back: Divided

The Brothers' Bungalow was built in 1898 and
demolished in 1929. It was situated at the site of
the present St. Patrick's School at Marine Parade
Road, near Katong.

Orig. Photo C. J. Kleingrothe, Medan 1906.

Singapore. The Sea View Hotel — Tennis-Court.

[400]

SINGAPORE. THE SEA VIEW HOTEL – TENNIS COURT. (1906)

Back: Divided
Publisher: C.J. Kleingrothe, Medan

Showing the Sea View Hotel and its tennis court set amidst coconut trees by the seaside. The postcard is dated 1906 on its picture side. The message side stated that W. Percy Spiers was the proprietor of the hotel.

SEA VIEW HOTEL

SEA VIEW HOTEL-TANJONG KATONG, SINGAPORE.

[401]

SEA VIEW HOTEL – TANJONG KATONG, SINGAPORE. (C 1910)

Back: Divided
Publisher: Koh & Co., Singapore

A view of the Sea View Hotel from the front of the beach. The hotel had a landing pier (postcard's right hand side); this allowed guests to travel from Johnston's Pier in town to the hotel.

Chinese village Tompson Rd.

W. Windrath
SINGAPORE.
Straits Settlements

238

[406]
CHINESE VILLAGE TOMPSON RD. (C 1900)

Cancellation: 1901
Back: Undivided

The word "Thomson" is spelt wrongly as "Tompson". W. Windrath was a well-known stamp dealer in the early 1900s.

Singapore, Serembang. Market.

158

[407]
SINGAPORE, SEREMBANG. MARKET. (C 1910)

Back: Divided
Publisher: Max H. Hilckes, Singapore

The word Sembawang is also spelt wrongly as "Serembang".

[408]
PONGGOL, SINGAPORE. (1932)

Cancellation: 1933
Back: Divided

A photographic postcard of Ponggol (now spelt as Punggol) with its coastline dotted with coconut trees.

[409]
BEDOH SINGAPORE. (C 1930)

Back: Divided

A photographic postcard of the Bedoh (now spelt as Bedok) beach around 1930.

Singapore—Passir Panjang.   Sea Side

[410]]
SINGAPORE – PASSIR PANJANG. SEA SIDE.
(C 1930)

Back: Divided
Series and/or No.: Sandbridge/39
Publisher: J. Brignon

Showing the long sandy beach at Pasir Panjang.

HAW PAR VILLA - SINGAPORE

[411]
HAW PAR VILLA. SINGAPORE. (C 1940)

Back: Divided

The Haw Par Villa was built by the Aw Brothers (Boon Par and Boon Haw) in 1937 and was part of Tiger Balm Garden.

St. John's Island, Singapore.

[412]
St. John's Island, Singapore. (c 1920)

Back: Divided
Publisher: German

St. John's Island was a lazaretto (quarantine station/infectious diseases hospital) from 1874 to 1978. It is about 6.5 km south of Singapore.

On the sea shore Blakang Mati Singapore.

[413]
On the sea shore Blakang Mati Singapore. (c 1907)

Cancellation: 1907
Back: Undivided
Publisher: Hartwig & Co., Succ., Singapore

It was used by the British Military as a hospital during the Colonial Days. In 1972, it was renamed "Sentosa" (Isle of peace and tranquility) and revamped into a resort and theme park.

[414]
PULOE BRANI FERRY – SINGAPORE. (C 1912)

Cancellation: 1912
Back: Divided
Series and/or No.: 43
Publisher: The Continental Stamp Company, Singapore

In the postcard's background is Pulau Blakang Mati (Sentosa Island).

[415]
SINGAPORE. PULAU BUKUM. (C 1910)

Back: Divided

Pulau Bukum was then a desolated Malay fishing village and a source of fresh water for ships.

View from the Kramat Hill - Koosoo Island.

[416]
VIEW FROM KRAMAT HILL – KOOSOO ISLAND.
(C 1910)

Back: Divided
Series and/or No.: 225
Publisher: Max H. Hilckes, Singapore

The *tua peh kong* temple is in centre of the postcard.

Raffles Lighthouse, Singapore.

[417]
RAFFLES LIGHTHOUSE, SINGAPORE. (1907)

Cancellation: 1907
Back: Divided

The Raffles Lighthouse was built in 1856 on Coney Island (now known as Pulau Satumu). Today it is known for the many pristine diving sites around it.

MULTIRACIAL SINGAPORE

A multiview postcard of 13 views showing the Malays, Chinese and Indians in Singapore around 1898.
(*See* [418])

A Nonya posing besides a large Chinese porcelain vase around 1900.
(*See* [422])

Multiracial Singapore

"Singapore is now, and since its foundation always has been, one of the most cosmopolitan cities in the world. In 1897, it contained 27 or more nationalities. In the 1911 census, no less than 54 different languages were recorded as being spoken in the settlement and 48 different races (counting Chinese and Indian as only one each) were represented."[29]

At its foundation in 1819, the population of Singapore amounted to about 150 individuals. About 30 of them were Chinese and the rest, Malays who had accompanied the Temenggong when he settled in Singapore in 1811.[29]

The town of Singapore grew very quickly after 1819 – in 1821, the population was estimated at 4,727. By 1860, the population had swelled to 81,734. Today, according to the July 2003 census estimation, the population of Singapore has now reached 4.6 million![70]

The multiracial people of Singapore at around 1900 are well illustrated [418 (*left, top*); 419] and they are further elaborated upon below.

The Chinese

Soon after Sir Stamford Raffles founded Singapore in 1819, many Malays and Chinese migrated from Malacca to Singapore. On 11 June 1819, Sir Stamford wrote to the Duchess of Somerset: "My new colony thrives most rapidly. We have not been established for months, and it has received an accession of population exceeding 5,000 – principally Chinese, and their number is daily increasing."[33]

Many of such Chinese migrants were termed Peranakans (a Malay word that applies to those who are native by birth)[72]. A Peranakan male is called a Baba while his female equivalent is called a Nonya [422 (*left, middle*)]. Terms like Straits Chinese, Straits-born Chinese, Baba Chinese or Peranakan are simply terms which have been used interchangeably. By and large, the Singapore's Baba community was an extension of that of Malacca.[72]

The identity of the Peranakan, like their speech, tended to be a cultural blend of Chinese (Hokkien), Malay and British. The Peranakans sent their children to English schools; they developed a rapport with the Europeans which resulted in them adopting westernised habits and business procedures. They were favoured by the colonial masters and they prospered in their businesses (trading, opium[41], plantations, shipping etc.). They also displayed their wealth ostentatiously – they built big bungalows and villas and they commissioned porcelain from China (nonya wares) and Europe.[73] They adored beautiful and elaborate jewellery in silver, gold and diamonds and other objet d'art [420; 421].

The Peranakans loved English music and formed musical bands, such as the Cornwall Minstrels [423]. They were also active in sports, as many of them took up English sporting activities [426].

However, many of the early migrants from China led hard lives; they worked as rickshaw pullers, servants and labourers, and lived in squalor in Chinatown [428; 429]. The Chinese migrants in Singapore were mainly Buddhists; they built many temples; one of biggest and oldest is the "Siong Lim Temple" built by the Hokkiens in Jalan Toa Payoh [430].

Many of the early Chinese migrants were Cantonese [424] from South China. When the Chinese prospered, some of them bought titles (ranks) from the Qing Government in China [425]. However, they celebrated the Lunar New Year with Chingay processions [427], while lavish funeral processions were held for the rich Chinese [431].

The Malays

The Pangkor Treaty of 1874 defined the Malay as an individual who speaks the Malay language, proclaims faith in Islam and practises the Malay culture. Later, the term "Malay" was expanded to include everyone from the Nasantara "the Malaya-Indonesian Archipelago"[67]. At its foundation in 1819, Singapore had a population of about 150, of which 120 (80%) were Malays.[29] In the 1911 census, Singapore had a population of 303,321; of these 41,932 (13.8%) were Malays belonging to various Malay races (i.e. Javanese, Boyanese, Bugis and Achehnese, etc.)[29] [432-437].

Many of the Malay races lived along the rivers and coastline [433 (right, top)]. The flourishing trade in Singapore also attracted many Javanese who eventually settled down in Singapore. They were mostly employed as plantation workers and drivers; their number increased with the development of rubber estates after 1910. The Malays of early Singapore were generally well known to be either fishermen [438] or postmen [439]. In prewar Singapore, however, there were also many Malay policemen and street vendors.

The Indians

"The Indians of the Malabar and Coromandel coast stood next to the Chinese, and of the Asiatic population come nearest to that industrious people in usefulness and intelligence."[29]

In 1821, the Indian population of Singapore was only 132, and by 1911, the Indian races formed 23,770 (9.2%) of Singapore's then total population of 303,321. Of these, 4,544 were described as Straits-born while the rest were Indian migrants[29], of which most of them were males (the migrations of women and children became common only after 1930). The majority of these migrants came from South India, but there were also large numbers from

what are today known as North India, Pakistan, Bangladesh and Sri Lanka.[63] The 2000 census of Singapore showed that 7.6% of its population (4.6 million) were Indians.[70]

Many of the early Indian migrants settled in Serangoon Road and its vicinity while the Malay-Arab-Indian migrants congregated at Kampong Glam.[63] Indian migrants worked in rubber and tea plantations. They built roads, railways, telecommunications and municipal buildings. The more fortunate Indian migrants became clerks and junior administrators in the colonial bureaucracy.[63]

An Indian juggler is shown in [440]; likewise Tamil actors in [442] and a workman in [443].

The Europeans and the other races

Two years after the founding of Singapore in 1821, Singapore's total population was estimated to be around 4,727; of which 29 were Europeans. By 1823, however, these numbers had increased significantly and there were no less than nine European mercantile houses. The 1911 census reflected that of the total population then (303,321), 5,711 were Europeans. Two well known Englishmen in the early 1900s are shown in [444; 445] However, among the many minority races in Singapore in 1911 were Japanese (1,409), Arabs (1,226), Jews (595), Singhalese (169), Siamese (149), etc.[29]

In the late 1800s and early 1900s, many Japanese women worked as *karayuki-san* (Japanese prostitutes in "Little Japan" (Malay Street area).[46] In the 1900s, there was also a small community of Siamese; a group of Siamese monks in Singapore in 1904 is shown [441 (right, middle)]. The Eurasians were not categorised in the early census of Singapore[29]; nevertheless their presence is indicated by their club, the Singapore Recreation Club at the Padang [130].

The Malays, Orang Lauts, Boyanese and other Malay races often lived in stilt houses along the coasts and rivers. This picture was taken in 1923. (*See* [433])

A group of Siamese monks in Singapore posing outside a Siamese Monastery in 1904. (*See* [441])

245

[418]
SINGAPORE. (C 1898)

Cancellation: 1901
Back: Undivided
Publisher: G.R. Lambert & Co., Singapore

A multiview postcard of 13 views showing the Malays, Chinese and Indians in Singapore. The postcard is tinted in beautiful colours, and it is a masterpiece of G.R. Lambert.

[419]
GREETINGS FROM SINGAPORE. (C 1900)

Cancellation: 1900
Back: Undivided
Publisher: C.A. Ribeiro & Co., Singapore

This azure-toned multiview postcard shows views of a "Chilty, Tamil Woman, Javanese Merchant, Malay Policeman, Malay Woman and Sikh Policeman" amidst palm trees.

[420]

SINGAPORE. CHINESE WOMAN. (1913)

Cancellation: 1913
Back: Divided
Series and/or No.: 117
Publisher: Max H. Hilckes, Singapore

Showing a young Peranakan woman sitting in a studio and posing in a long dress (*baju panjang*) and beaded slippers.

[421]

Untitled [A beautiful young Nonya]. (c 1930)

Back: Divided

A portrait of a beautiful young Nonya wearing elaborate diamond jewelleries: her floral crown is secured by diamond hairpins; her *baju panjang* is fastened with 3 brooches (*kerogsangs*) and she wears earrings, collar studs and necklaces.

[422]

A STRAITS CHINESE GIRL. (C 1910)

Back: Divided
Publisher: G.R. Lambert & Co., Singapore

A Nonya posing besides a large Chinese porcelain vase.

[423]

SINGAPORE. THE CORNWALL MINSTRELS – (STRAITS CHINESE AMATEURS). (1909)

Cancellation: 1911
Back: Divided

The 5th anniversary celebrations of the Cornwall Minstrels held in the house of its President (Mr. Kuek Beng Chiew) at Tanjong Katong in 1909.[21]

[424]
CANTONESE GIRL – SINGAPORE. (1908)

Cancellation: 1908
Back: Divided

A Cantonese girl wearing a *samfoo* attire posing by a table with a covered Chinese porcelain tea-cup and water pipe on it.

[425]
SINGAPORE. MANDARIN. (C 1906)

Cancellation: 1906
Back: Undivided

Buying his title from the Qing Government in China, the Mandarin in the postcard is wearing his badge of rank. The Federated Malay States 1¢ stamp was cancelled in Singapore.

[426]
CHINESE NEW YEAR SPORTS, SINGAPORE.
(C 1900)

Cancellation: 1908
Back: Divided
Publisher: Koh & Co., Singapore

Depicts activities held during the Chinese New Year at Hong Lim Green along South Bridge Road. Many of the Chinese had hair queues and they wore Chinese and British-style hats.

[427]
SINGAPORE. CHINESE CHINGAY PROCESSION.
(1910)

Cancellation: 1910
Back: Divided

Such depicted processions of brightly and elaborately decorated floats were held on the 15th day of the Chinese New Year, or on the birthday of the deity Kuan Yin.

Chinese workmen at dinner.

Chinese Ice Cream seller.

[428]
CHINESE WORKMEN AT DINNER. (C 1910)

Back: Divided
Publisher: G.R. Lambert & Co., Singapore

This photographic postcard shows a group of Chinese
workmen having a meal outside a dilapidated wooden house.

[429]
CHINESE ICE CREAM SELLER. (C 1910)

Back: Divided
Publisher: G.R. Lambert & Co., Singapore

A Chinese ice-cream seller using a push cart and
ringing a bell to announce his presence.

[430]
CHINESE TEMPLE BALLESTIER ROAD, SINGAPORE.
(1919)

Cancellation: 1919
Back: Divided
Publisher: Koh & Co., Singapore

A postcard showing the Siong Lim Temple in
Jalan Toa Payoh (the Lohan Hall).

[431]
SINGAPORE. CHINESE FUNERAL PARTY. (1901)

Cancellation: 1901
Back: Undivided

A scene of a lavish funeral procession for the
rich. Such funeral processions were the norm in
prewar Singapore.

[432]
SINGAPORE. GROUP OF NATIVES. (C 1910)

Back: Divided
Series and/or No.: 1553
Publisher: Wilson & Co., Orchard Road, Singapore

This postcard shows a portrait of a Boyanese family.

[433]
MALAY GIRLS, SINGAPORE. (1923)

Cancellation: 1923
Back: Divided
Series and/or No.: 6
Publisher: K.P. Hock, Singapore

The Malays, Orang Lauts, Boyanese and other Malay races often lived in stilt houses along the coast and rivers.

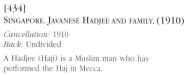

254

[434]
SINGAPORE. JAVANESE HADJEE AND FAMILY. (1910)

Cancellation: 1910
Back: Undivided

A Hadjee (Haji) is a Muslim man who has
performed the Haj in Mecca.

[435]
MALAY WOMAN. (1912)

Cancellation: 1912
Back: Divided

The young lady in the postcard is dressed typically in
a Malay dress (head scarf, *baju kurong* and slippers).

Group of Malay children   Singapore

G. R. Lambert & Co. Gresham House, Singapore

[436]
GROUP OF MALAY CHILDREN SINGAPORE.
(1903)

Cancellation: 1903
Back: Undivided
Publisher: G.R. Lambert & Co., Singapore

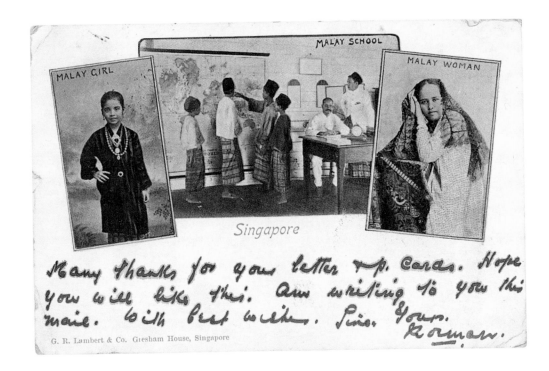

MALAY GIRL   MALAY SCHOOL   MALAY WOMAN

Singapore

G. R. Lambert & Co. Gresham House, Singapore

[437]
SINGAPORE. (1903)

Cancellation: 1903
Back: Undivided
Publisher: G.R. Lambert & Co., Singapore

A multiview postcard depicting a Malay Girl, a Malay School and a Malay Woman.

Malay Fishermen.

W. Windrath
SINGAPORE.
Straits Settlements

[438]
MALAY FISHERMEN. (C 1900)

Back: Undivided

A group of Malay fishermen are drying their fishing nets besides their boats.

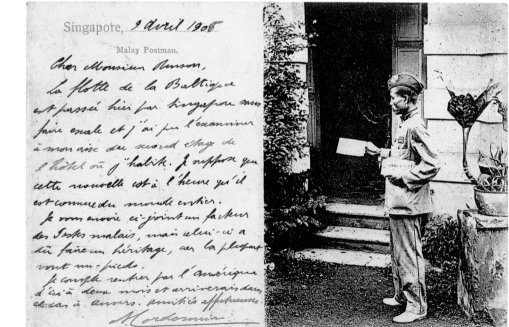

Malay Postman.

[439]
SINGAPORE, MALAY POSTMAN. (1905)

Cancellation: 1905
Back: Undivided

A Malay postman delivering a letter; in those days letters were delivered by hand and the postman walked from house to house.

[440]

SINGAPORE. (C 1898)

Back: Divided
Publisher: Not stated. Attributed to Kunzli Freres, Zurich

Showing an ink-sketched and coloured postcard of an Indian juggler and his two performing monkeys.

[441]

SINGAPORE. (1904)

Cancellation: 1904
Back: Undivided

In this postcard, a group of Siamese monks in Singapore is shown posing outside a Siamese Monastery.

[442]
TAMIL ACTORS. (1912)

Cancellation: 1912
Back: Divided
Series and/or No.: 63

Depicts a travelling group of entertainers comprising Tamil actors and musicians.

[443]
STRAITS SETTLEMENTS. (1930)

Cancellation: 1930
Back: Divided

An Indian man is painted standing besides his printing press.

H. E. Sir John Anderson, K.C.M.G., *Governor of Straits Settlements.*

This is a very good likeness of His Excellency! He is home on Holiday. Love to all from Amy

No. 23 | British Empire Series

7

Extension of original plantation on old Para rubber

[444]
**H.E. SIR JOHN ANDERSON, K.C.M.G., GOVERNOR OF STRAITS
SETTLEMENTS. (C 1906)**

Cancellation: 1906
Back: Undivided
Series and/or No.: British Empire Series, No. 23

A portrait of Sir John Anderson (Governor, Straits Settlements,
1904–1911). He is the only governor to be featured on a postcard.

[445]
Untitled [H.N Ridley in the Botanic Gardens]. (c 1905)

Back: Undivided
Publisher: G.R. Lambert & Co., Singapore

H.N Ridley standing on the left side of one of the rubber
trees he planted at the Botanic Gardens. He had a thick
moustache and was dressed formally with a hat and cane.

MODES of TRANSPORTATION

Tank Road Railway Station and its vicinity around 1912.
(*See* [452])

The Singapore Railway station around 1935.
(*See* [457])

Sea Transportation

"The maritime heritage of Singapore was well established long before the founding vision of Sir Stamford Raffles rescued this small island from the obscurity with his historic landing on 28 January 1819. While history is vague about how this island of topical forest and coastal mangrove developed from a settlement into a port, the sheltered waterway of Temasek ("sea town") harbour was already known to mariners who called on this settlement… more than a thousand years ago."[28]

Singapore lies 88 miles North of the Equator; it has been called "an emporium for British trade in the East Indies" and "the Gibraltar of the East", for "Enlightened vision and planning had led to the rise of Singapore as an entrepot serving the region and beyond."[28] Boat yards to service and repair vessels were set up at Telok Ayer. By 1822, a total of 139 vessels were recorded.

However, by the mid-1800s, Collyer Quay and the Old Harbour had become too congested (due to the increase in sea traffic) while its entrance became too narrow for ocean steamers. To deal with these problems, the Keppel Harbour (New Harbour) was opened in 1852. More importantly, the Keppel Harbour had been constructed in such a way that it was now linked to the rivers by roads. This meant that the imports from riverine activities could now be transported to become exports for sea-borne trade and vice-versa. The transshipment trade, which later grew in size and sophistication, originated from this period onward. The arrival of steamers was a bonus for the development of the port, as it gave rise to coal bunkering, the fore-runner of today's oil refining and bunkering industries.[28]

In the 1900s, many international and regional liners called at Singapore: Blue Funnel Line, the P. & O., Glen, Ben and City Lines, Messageries Maritimes, Nippon Yusen Kaisha, Netherland Royal Mail, Rotterdam Lloyd, East Asiatic, Lloyd Triestino, etc.

Many of the above passenger liners distributed ppcs of their port of call [450; 451]. Two such early ppcs of Singapore (c 1900) produced by the Hamburg Amerika Line are produced from watercolour paintings of Kampong Bahru [446] and the Sri Mariamman Temple on South Bridge Road [447]. Ppcs of Singapore with humorous pictures are uncommon; two such ppcs produced by the French Shipping Line, Messageries Maritimes, are shown in [448; 449].

In less than two centuries, Singapore has progressed from an entrepot to a technoport, from a warehousing centre to a global distriport, and from a fishing village to the world's busiest port.[28]

Rail Transportation

The Singapore Railway was built in 1903 after much debate, for as early as 1869, plans to build a railway had been underway but not carried out. In 1909, the line that linked Singapore to the Malayan hinterland right up to Prai was completed. In 1918, the properties and roads of the Singapore Railway were sold to the Government of the Federated Malay States; it was then known as the Federated Malay States Railway (F.M.S.R.).[74]

The Tank Road Railway Station [452 (*left, top*)] was the only terminal station for passengers; it was opened on 1 January 1903. In 1903, the train ran from Cuppage Road [453] (behind Orchard Road) to Newton [454] and Woodlands [455]. From there, passengers wishing to continue on to Malaya were then carried across the Johore Straits by launches [455]. However, this Railway Station closed down in 1932.[4,74]

The causeway linking Singapore to Johore [456] was opened in 1923. The Railway Station [457 (*left, middle*)] at Tanjong Pagar belonging to the F.M.S.R. was constructed in 1932, and its trains ran from Tanjong Pagar across the causeway to Johore.

The F.M.S.R. Station Building at Tanjong Pagar was completed in 1932 and it has a fine central waiting hall with a curved roof. The walls are decorated with typical Malayan scenes such as rice planting, rubber tapping, shipping activities, bullock transportation, coconut growing and tin mining.[9]

Road Transportation

In prewar Singapore, bullock-carts [459] were used commonly to transport goods for short distances. They were also used to carry goods from the river banks and wharves into town, and at times, conservancy vehicles as well. Though a clumsy and inefficient means of transport, it provided an essential service before motorisation was introduced.[74]

The jinricksha (rickshaw) was imported from Japan in the 1880s. It was a very popular and cheap means of transport; the fare was 3¢ for half a mile or less, or 20¢ for an hour. The rickshaw pullers provided a much needed service and rickshaws continued to be used until a few years after the Second World War, with the main rickshaw stations being located at Neil Road and in Chinatown. Rickshaws finally faded out of service after the introduction of the trishaw in 1947.[74]

The horse and carriage [458 (*right, top*)], an English gentleman's means of travel, was a common sight in prewar Singapore. However, there were also smaller carriages used for hire; these were called "hackneys" or "gharries" which crowded the streets in the business area of town.[74]

In 1867, the steam train began running in Singapore; it was a commercial failure and was discontinued in 1894. The electric tram [459–461] was introduced in 1905 by the Singapore Electric Tramways Company; it functioned from 1905 to 1927. Six lines were laid to run

through town and it carried an average of 11,000 passengers a day at height of its service.[74]

Singapore's first car was imported in 1896 for a prominent Englishman named Charles Burton Buckley; although its numbers grew slowly, by the 1930s, their numbers had grown phenomenally, and they gradually replaced the use of the horse and carriage. Motor trucks, lorries and vans gradually replaced the old bullock-carts for the transport of goods and services.[74]

Air Transportation

A pictorial review of civil aviation in Singapore from 1911 to 1981 has been published in "Singapore Fly-Past".[75] Aviation was introduced to Singapore on 4 March 1911 when Joseph Christiaens, a Frenchman, landed his Bristol Box-Kite biplane at the Race Course in Farrer Park [462] after a 22-day flight from England. Eight years later in 1919, Ross Smith, an Australian, landed his Vickers Army airplane in Singapore on a pioneering flight from England to Australia.[75] The first passengers to arrive in Singapore in a chartered KLM aircraft landed at Balestier Plain in 1927, and subsequent aircrafts landed at the Royal Air Force airfield at Seletar.

Kallang Airport [463–465] was constructed by reclaiming mangrove swamp and land from the sea[9]; it was officially opened on 12 June 1937. The interior of the terminal building [464 (*right, middle*)] was "extraordinary in terms of design taste and the last gasp of Art-Deco".[74] Two weeks after its opening, Malaya's first internal air service from Singapore to Kuala Lumpur and Penang (Wearne's Air Services) was inaugurated.

During the postwar period, Paya Lebar Airport replaced Kallang Airport in the 1950s, which in turn was superseded by Changi International Airport in 1981. The growth of civil aviation in the modern era has been phenomenal; few could have foretold the progress of aviation in Singapore since the time Joseph Christiaens first landed his primitive biplane at Farrer Park in 1911!

A traffic jam along Collyer Quay caused by horses and carriages, around 1905. (*See* [458])

The Art-Deco interior of the terminus building in the Kallang Airport in 1937. (*See* [464])

261

[446]
SINGAPORE (KAMPONG BAHRU). (C 1900)

Back: Undivided
Publisher: J. Aberle, Berlin

A postcard showing a watercolour painting of Malay houses and fishing boats.

[447]
SINGAPORE KLING TEMPEL. (C 1900)

Back: Undivided
Publisher: J. Aberle, Berlin

A watercolour postcard painting depicting the Sri Mariamman Temple in South Bridge Road.

[448]

SINGAPORE. LE COIFFEUR CHINOIS. [SINGAPORE. THE CHINESE
HAIRDRESSER.] (C 1910)

Cancellation: Nil
Back: Divided
Publisher: Imp. Hermieu, Paris

A humorous postcard produced by the French Shipping Company,
Messageries Maritimes. It consists a watercolour painting of a
street-side Chinese barber digging the ear of a customer.

[449]

SINGAPORE. EXCES DE VITESSE. [SINGAPORE. TRAVELLING
AT AN EXCESS SPEED.] (C 1910)

Back: Divided
Publisher: Imp. Hermieu, Paris

Produced also by Messageries Martimes, this postcard
shows a Sikh policeman stopping a speeding rickshaw
puller who has an European lady in his rickshaw.

SINGAPORE CHINEEZEN.

Singapore Chinese family

KONINKLIJKE PAKETVAART - MAATSCHAPPIJ
(ROYAL DUTCH PACKET COMPANY)

[450]
SINGAPORE CHINEEZEN. [SINGAPORE CHINESE.]
(C 1920)

Back: Divided

A photographic postcard of a Chinese family
produced by the Royal Dutch Packet Company.
The postcard has a serrated lower edge; it is likely
to be have been detached from a menu card.

NEESOON & SONS, LIMITED.
RUBBER WORKS, NEESOON VILLAGE,
SELETAR, SINGAPORE, S.S.

Cable Address:
"MARSILING" Singapore.

U. S. A. Sole Agents:
Messrs. Oliver, Keeler & Scudder.,
24, Stone Street,
NEW YORK.

[451]
NEE SOON & SONS LIMITED. RUBBER WORKS,
NEESOON VILLAGE, SELETAR, SINGAPORE, S.S.
(1923)

Cancellation: 1923
Back: Divided

A photographic postcard of the Nee Soon & Sons
Limited Rubber Works at Seletar, Singapore. On
the back of the postcard was stamped "With
Compliments/to our American Visitors
(Tourists)/per S/S "SAMARIA" from/Neeson &
Sons, Limited/Singapore, S.S. 25–26 March 1923".

Tank Road Station and its Visinity, Singapore.   No. 16

[452]
TANK ROAD STATION AND ITS VISINITY, SINGAPORE. (C 1910)

Back: Divided
Series and/or No.: 16
Publisher: Japanese

This was Singapore's main rail terminus from 1903 to 1932.

Orchard Road Railway Bridge - Singapore

[453]
ORCHARD ROAD RAILWAY BRIDGE –
SINGAPORE. (C 1910)

Back: Divided
Series and/or No.: 3
Publisher: The Continental Stamp Company, Singapore

This view of the Orchard Road Railway Bridge looks northwards and shows the Orchard Road Railway Bridge near Emerald Hill.

Newton Station, Singapore.

[454]
NEWTON STATION, SINGAPORE. (C 1910)

Back: Divided
Publisher: Kong Hing Chiong & Co., North Bridge Road, Singapore

K.D. 14.11.'09   Singapore-Johore Railway Ferryboat Johore Jetty.

[455]
SINGAPORE – JOHORE RAILWAY FERRYBOAT JOHORE JETTY. (1907)

Cancellation: 1907
Back: Undivided
Publisher: Hartwig & Co., Succ., Singapore

Passengers from the Tank Road Railway Station stopped here and were ferried to Johore Bahru to continue their railway journey up-country.

JOHORE CAUSEWAY

[456]

JOHORE CAUSEWAY. (c 1923)

Back: Divided

A photographic postcard of the Johore Causeway, which was more than 1000 metres long. The Causeway was opened in 1923.

13   Singapore Station of F. M. S. Railways.

[457]

SINGAPORE STATION OF F.M.S. RAILWAYS. (c 1935)

Back: Divided

The Singapore Station at Keppel Road was built in 1932; the train service ran between here and Johore Bahru. The station is still functioning today.

Crowded Collyer Quay. Singapore.

[458]
CROWDED COLLYER QUAY. SINGAPORE. (C 1905)

Back: Undivided
Publisher: Hartwig & Co., Succ., Singapore

A traffic jam along Collyer Quay, which was caused by horses and carriages!

TRAVEL BY TROLLEY BUS AND SAVE YOUR MONEY

Local Traffic, Singapore

[459]
LOCAL TRAFFIC, SINGAPORE. (1934)

Cancellation: 1934
Back: Divided

A photographic postcard of the traffic along North Bridge Road at its junction with Stamford Road. A bullock-cart, rickshaws, a trolley bus and many cars are seen in this postcard.

Electric Tramway Power Station, Singapore.

[460]

ELECTRIC TRAMWAY POWER STATION, SINGAPORE. (C 1910)

Back: Divided

The Electric Tramway Power Station was situated at MacKenzie Road, off Bukit Timah Road. It supplied power for the electric trams that ran from 1905 to 1927.

Traffic Policeman on Duty, Singapore.

[461]

TRAFFIC POLICEMAN ON DUTY, SINGAPORE. (C 1925)

Back: Divided

The Sikh traffic policeman is dressed in a turban and a khaki uniform with rattan arms directing traffic at the junction of North Bridge Road and Bras Basah Road.

Aviation Meeting (Race Course) March 1911.

[462]
AVIATION MEETING (RACE COURSE) MARCH 1911.

Back: Divided
Series and/or No.: 294
Publisher: Max H. Hilckes, Singapore

Joseph Christiaens landed his Bristol Box-Kite biplane at the Race Course in Farrer Park on 4 March 1911.

D 13   AERODROME S'PORE

[463]
AERODROME S'PORE. (1937)

Cancellation: Nil
Back: Divided
Series and/or No.: D 13

A photographic postcard of the Kallang Airport at its opening on 12 June 1937.

[464]

AIR PORT SINGAPORE. (1937)

Back: Divided

A photographic postcard of the Art-Deco interior of the terminus building in the Kallang Airport.

[465]

SINGAPORE AIRPORT. (c 1938)

Back: Divided

This postcard shows a Quantas Empire Airways plane (RMA Brisbane) parked at the Kallang Airport.

ROYAL EVENTS and EXHIBITIONS

The Duke of Connaught's visit to Singapore in 1906.
(*See* [467])

The visit of the Prince of Wales to Singapore in 1922.
(*See* [468])

Visit of the Duke and Duchess of York (1901)

The Duke and Duchess of York (the future King George V and Queen Mary) visited Singapore on 22 April 1901. The royal couple drove from Johnston's Pier to the Government House [466]. The visit of the royal couple included a rickshaw ride through Chinatown and the couple was presented with an album of 100 photographs from the firm of G.R. Lambert.[29]

Visit of the Duke and Duchess of Connaught (1906)

The visit of the Duke and Duchess of Connaught to Singapore in 1906 [467 (*left, top*)] was celebrated with spectacular arches, brilliant lanterns and illuminated dragons. A flower show was held and Whampoa and Choa Kim Keat figured among the prize-winners.[33]

Visit of the Prince of Wales (1922)

His Royal Highness, the Prince of Wales, K.G. (the future King Edward VIII) visited Singapore from 31 October to 1 April 1922.[76] On arrival in Singapore, his Royal Highness was welcomed by thousands of schoolchildren [468 (*left, middle*)]. The route taken by the Prince was lined with several arches (illuminated at night); the arch erected by the Indian and Ceylonese communities across Orchard Road outside the Presbyterian Church is shown in [469]. One of the highlights of the Prince's stay in Singapore was a visit to the Malaya Borneo Exhibition [470] on 31 March 1922.[76] Stamps of the Straits Settlements [500], Kedah, Kelantan, Brunei and North Borneo were specially overprinted for this exhibition.

Silver Jubilee of King George V (1935)

The public celebrations in honour of the Silver Jubilee of His Majesty King George V took place in Singapore from 6 to 11 May 1935.[77] At 7:30 am on 6 May 1935, a Ceremonial Parade was held at the Padang [471]. There was a lantern procession, fireworks and beating of the Retreat by the Band and Drums of the 1st Batallion, the Wiltshire Regimen.[77]

Coronation of King George VI (1937)

The coronation of King George VI took place in London on 12 May 1937 and was celebrated in Singapore with many illuminated arches across the streets; such an arch in the vicinity of the Victoria Theatre is shown in [472].

Agri-Horticultural Shows

The first Agri-Horticultural show was held in Kuala Lumpur in 1904; the second in Penang in 1905 and the third in Singapore in 1906 from 6 to 8 August. The Governor, Sir John Anderson, performed the opening ceremony at all the three shows. Two of the exhibitors at the 1906 show are shown in [474; 475].[33]

British Empire Exhibition (1924–1925)

The British Empire Exhibition was held at Wembley, England from 23 April to 1 November 1924 and reopened from 9 May to 31 October 1925.[78] Malaya (and Singapore) had a pavilion in the overseas section, which featured all the colonies of the British Empire. The purpose of the exhibition was to showcase the industrial activities of England and all phases of life of the British colonies.[78]

The Malaya pavilion sold black and white real photographic ppcs of Malaya and Singapore [473]. The ppcs were published for the Malayan Government and produced in Singapore. Most of the ppcs were not used; a few were used at Wembley; there were more Malayan than Singapore ppcs.

[466]
Untitled [Visit of the Duke and Duchess of York]. (1901)

Cancellation: 1901
Back: Undivided

The Duke and Duchess of York visited Singapore on 22 April 1901; they rode in a horse carriage from Johnston's Pier to Government House.

Duke of Connaught's Visit, Singapore.

[467]
DUKE OF CONNAUGHT'S VISIT, SINGAPORE. (1906)

Back: Divided

The royal retinue was led by Sikh horsemen; a welcome arch is visible in the background.

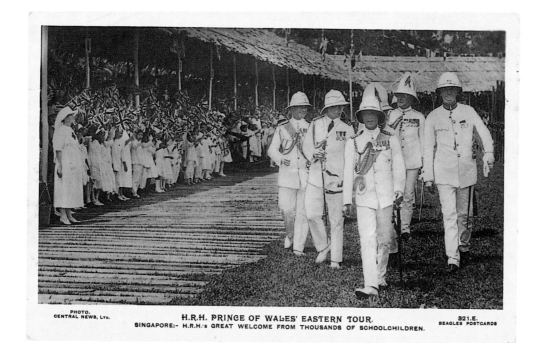

[468]
H.R.H. PRINCE OF WALES' EASTERN TOUR.
(1922)

Back: Divided
Publisher: J. Beagles & Co. Ltd., England

The Prince of Wales was welcomed by thousands of school children when he arrived in Singapore.

[469]
Untitled [Welcoming arch for the Prince of Wales]. (1922)

Back: Divided

A photographic postcard showing the arch erected across Orchard Road outside the Presbyterian Church by the Indian and Ceylonese communities to welcome the Prince of Wales.

[470]

GREETINGS FROM SINGAPORE.

Back: Divided
Series and/or No.: 6
Publisher: Koh & Co., Singapore

A multiview photocard of the ladies of the various ethnic groups in Singapore. The address side of the postcard was overprinted "H.R.H. The Prince of Wales/Visits Singapore/The Malaya - Borneo/Exhibition/31st March 1922".

[471]

Untitled [Leaving the Padang after a Ceremonial Parade]. (1935)

Back: Divided

A scene depicting the crowds leaving the Padang after watching a Ceremonial Parade which marked the Silver Jubilee of King George V.

[472]

Untitled [An illuminated arch]. (1937)

Back: Divided

Showing an illuminated arch celebrating the coronation of King George VI. The Victoria Theatre is discernable in the background.

[473]

VICTORIA MEMORIAL HALL AND THEATRE, SINGAPORE.

Cancellation: 1924
Back: Divided
Series and/or No.: 9239
Publisher: Houghton Butcher (Eastern) Ltd., "Camera House", Robinson Road, Singapore

A photographic postcard of Singapore that was sold at the 1924 British Empire Exhibition at the Malayan Pavilion in Wembly, England. On the address side of the postcard were printed the words "British Empire Exhibition, 1924" and a lion logo of the Exhibition.

Agri - Horticultural Show, Singapore.

Agri-Horticultural Show, Singapore.

[474]

AGRI-HORTICULTURAL SHOW, SINGAPORE. (1906)

Back: Divided
Publisher: German

The third Agri-Horticultural Show showing the exhibit of Robinson & Co.

[475]

AGRI-HORTICULTURAL SHOW, SINGAPORE. (1906)

Back: Divided
Publisher: German

The stand of the East Asiatic Company (advertising Dahl's Milk) at the Agri-Horticultural Show.

PANORAMAS, MULTIVIEWS and BOOKLETS

A postcard with five views (Hindu Temple, Mohamedian and Chinese temples, Chinese Tiffin House, Johnston's Pier and a Malay woman). (*See* [487])

A postcard with seven views tinted in subtle colours. (*See* [489])

Panoramic Picture Postcards

An ordinary ppc measures 14 x 9 cm (5.5 x 3.5 inches) while a panoramic ppc has the same width but is two to four times longer (28 to 58 cm or 11.0 to 22.0 inches) i.e. it has two to four folds. Apart from a three-fold ppc illustrated in 1986,[5] there is no published account of the panoramic ppcs of Singapore. These cards are scarce; most are unused. The panoramic ppcs were folded for sending through the post; some of the unused cards exist in the unfolded state; others may be proofs. Ordinary ppcs seem to restrict our vision; panoramic ppcs satisfy our desire to take in a wider view. This explains why panoramic ppcs are eagerly sought after by collectors today. Currently there are three types of panoramic ppcs:

(A) Two-fold Panoramic Picture Postcards (28 cm or 11.0 inches long)
[482, 483, 484]
(B) Three-fold Panoramic Picture Postcards (42 cm or 16.5 inches long)
[480]
(C) Four-fold Panoramic Picture Postcards (56 cm or 22 inches long)
[481]

Multiview Picture Postcards

Multiview ppcs are well known to collectors. The master of ppcs and photographs with multiviews or vignettes in the early 1900s was the photographer/publisher G.R. Lambert. Most of the photographs with multiviews in "Twentieth Century Impressions of British Malaya" published in 1908[18] are the work of G.R. Lambert. His ppcs with multiviews are some of the most beautiful early ppcs of Singapore.

A simple way to classify the ppcs with multiviews is by the number of views (vignettes) in the ppc. The main views are counted; the small or minor ones are ignored. Some of the multiview ppcs have "diffuse" or continuous images; these are classified arbitrarily. The multiview ppcs in this book have been classified as below:

(A) Picture Postcards with two views
[18-19, 47, 49, 71, 74, 76, 81, 136, 148, 153, 192, 300-301, 338, 485]
(B) Picture Postcards with three views
[14, 16-17. 149-151, 197, 221, 287, 291, 437]
(C) Picture Postcards with four views
[15, 277, 486]
(D) Picture Postcards with five views
[470, 487, 488]
(E) Picture Postcards with six or more views
[6 (eight views),137 (eight views), 339 (seven views), 418 (thirteen views), 419 (six views), 489-490 (seven views), 491-492 (eight views)]
(F) The Multiview Picture Postcards published by Kunzli Frefres, Zurich. These early multiview ppcs [122, 138, 196, 440, 493, 494] were published by Kunzli Frefres, Zurich, Switzerland, in 1898. They were made from watercolour paintings in bright vivid colours; the multiviews on a card were often diffusely mixed such that it is difficult to count the number of views on a ppc. These early ppcs of Singapore are scenic and are among the most beautiful ppcs produced.

The address side of these ppcs have the Royal Coat of Arms printed in light brown; this practice was not approved by the Government; thus the practice was short-lived and not followed by other publishers in later years.

Picture Postcard Booklets

Ppc booklets (Ppcbls) are well known to collectors but they have not been classified or catalogued. The ppcbls were produced between 1910 to 1940; they are all in black and white, or in sepia (brown tone). Each booklet commonly has 12 ppcs but may contain up to 20 ppcs. The ppcs are usually stapled together but may also be stitched. Each ppc is detachable from the spine on the left; hence such a ppcbl ppc has a serrated left border. Each ppcbl measures about 6.1 x 3.7 inches. As the ppcbls were produced from 1910 onwards, all the ppcs in them have Divided-Backs. Some of the ppcbl have tracing paper separating the ppcs.

Ppcbls of Singapore are more common than that of Malaya; there are a few booklets that have a mixture of Singapore and Malaya ppcs. It is simplest to classify the ppcbls according to their publishers. A few examples of the ppcbls are illustrated below:

(A) Published by G.R. Lambert & Co., Singapore
[476]
(B) Published by Max H. Hilckes, Singapore
[477]
(C) Photos taken by M.S. Nakajima, Singapore
[478-479]

Unfortunately, many ppcbls do not have details of their publishers; these form the majority of the prewar ppcbls of Singapore.

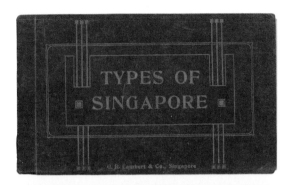

[476]
Publisher: G.R. Lambert & Co., Singapore (c 1910)

The cover is green with gold letterings. It was published by G.R. Lambert & Co., and contains 12 picture postcards in black and white.

[477]
Publisher: Max H. Hilckes, Singapore (c 1910)

The postcard booklet's cover has three peacocks on it, with the publisher's name inked in blue. It contained 20 black and white postcards; the picture postcards have interleaving tracing paper.

279

[478]
Publisher: M.S. Nakajima, Singapore (c 1910)

Black wordings framed by two thick black lines are distinguishable on the cover of this booklet. The postcards inside are in sepia-tone.

[479]
Publisher: M.S. Nakajima, Singapore (c 1920)

The cover of this postcard booklet is pink in colour and it is the third booklet in this series. It contained 12 picture postcards in sepia-tone.

21. x. 02. Hotel de l'Europe, Singapore.

This is about the best picture card I have seen. It gives a splendid idea
of Singapore. The centre of the town is on the right hand side. You can see what
a large place it really is. Note how much foliage there is in the town, and this really hides all the best buildings.

Panorama of Singapore
* Cathedral

23 juillet 1906 -

Panorama of Singapore from Fort Canning

petit père + ma chère petite mère.
joli panorama de Singapore en souvenir de mon séjour dans,
En même temps que ce petit paysage vous apporte le beau de votre
House, Singapore
venir 25 ans d'une bonne union que 3 restent

the signalling station at *Fort Channing*.
✕ Hotel de l'Europe   ✕ Canal wharf inside, Sea wharves outside,

dral alone stands out distinctly. Hope the post will not spoil it.   R.H.L.Lee

From top:

[480]

PANORAMA OF SINGAPORE. (1902)

Cancellation: 1902
Back: Undivided
Publisher: Not stated. Attributed to G.R. Lambert & Co., Singapore

This three-fold postcard offers a panoramic aerial view of Singapore taken from Fort Canning, with St. Andrew's Cathedral in the centre and the sea in its background. It was sent to London from the Hotel de l'Europe, Singapore.

[481]

PANORAMA OF SINGAPORE FROM FORT CANNING. (C 1900)

Back: Undivided
Publisher: G.R. Lambert & Co., Singapore

A rare four-fold panoramic postcard in bluish-grey tone of the breathtaking view of Singapore from the top of Fort Canning.

vos 25 ans de mariage. Je voudrais bien être près de vous deux pour ce joli jour qui marque sur le gr... s trois diables ont imposé pas[?] de durs sacrifices. Sauront ils jamais vous en récompenser plus tard, c... de tout mon cœur et ce a quoi je m'appliquerai toujours. votre grand...

Panorama of Singapore from the Sea Side (City)

G. R. Lambert & Co., Gresham House, Singapore

PANORAMA VIEW FROM THE SEA - SEAVIEW HOTEL. SINGAPORE.

Boat Quay, Singapore

Opposite (from top):

[482]

PANORAMA OF SINGAPORE FROM THE SEA SIDE (CITY). (C 1900)

Back: Undivided
Publisher: G.R. Lambert & Co., Singapore

A double-fold postcard showing the view of Fort Canning and Maxwell Market (left hand side) and Collyer Quay with sailing boats and tongkangs in the sea (right hand side).

[483]

PANORAMA VIEW FROM THE SEA. SEAVIEW HOTEL. SINGAPORE. (C 1930)

Back: Undivided
Publisher: Waterlow & Sons Limited, London, Dunstable and Waterford

A postcard with two folds, it shows a panoramic view of the sea from the Sea View Hotel.

[484]

BOAT QUAY, SINGAPORE. (C 1930)

Back: Divided
Publisher: Lim Swee Yak, Singapore

Printed in a sepia-tone, this double-fold panoramic postcard shows a bustling Boat Quay crowded with tongkangs and sampans.

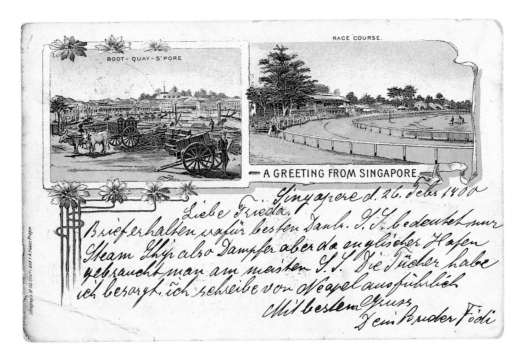

This page (from top):

[485]

A GREETING FROM SINGAPORE. (C 1900)

Cancellation: 1900
Back: Undivided
Publisher: Lithography of the Court I and P.A. Hasse, Prague

A double view postcard showing Boat Quay and the Race Course.

[486]

GREETING FROM SINGAPORE. (C 1900)

Cancellation: 1903
Back: Undivided
Publisher: Max Ludwig, Deutsche Buchhandlung, Singapore – Hong Kong.

A black on green background postcard with four views of the Singapore River and Drill Hall, the Istana at Kampong Glam, a riverine pier and the Raffles Hotel.

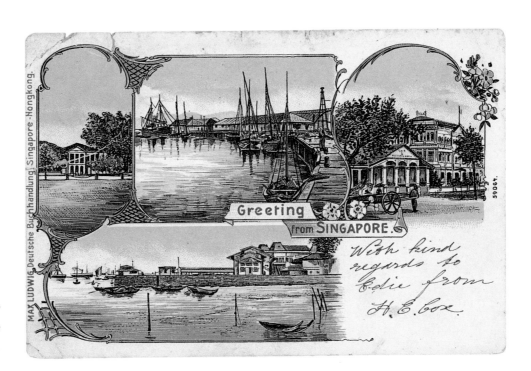

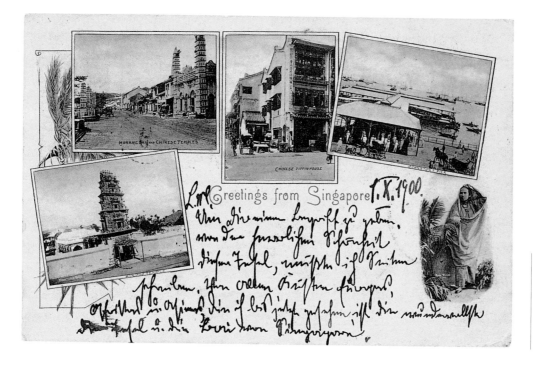

[487]
GREETINGS FROM SINGAPORE. (C 1900)

Cancellation: 1900
Back: Undivided
Publisher: Not stated. Attributed to G.R. Lambert & Co., Singapore

A postcard with five views (Hindu Temple, Mohamedian and Chinese temples, Chinese Tiffin House, Johnston's Pier and a Malay woman).

[488]
GREETINGS FROM SINGAPORE. (C 1900)

Cancellation: 1900
Back: Undivided
Publisher: Not stated. Attributed to G.R. Lambert & Co., Singapore

Like **[487]**, this coloured postcard has five views (Cavenagh Bridge, New Bridge Road, Boat Quay, Collyer Quay and a rickshaw with puller and client).

[489]
GREETINGS FROM SINGAPORE. (C 1900)

Cancellation: 1900
Back: Undivided
Publisher: Not stated. Attributed to G.R. Lambert & Co., Singapore

Presenting a postcard with seven views tinted in subtle colours.

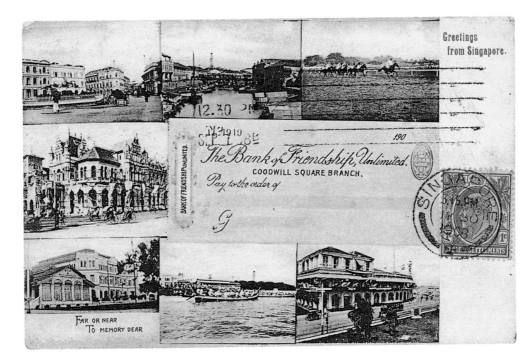

[490]
GREETINGS FROM SINGAPORE. (C 1900)

Cancellation: 1908
Back: Divided

This is a postcard with seven views that shows a number of famous landmarks in Singapore. On the postcard are printed the words "The Bank of Friendship Unlimited" (centre) and "Far or Near/ To Memory Dear" (left lower corner).

[491]
GREETINGS FROM SINGAPORE. (1899)

Cancellation: 1899
Back: Undivided
Publisher: G.R. Lambert & Co., Singapore

A colour-tinted postcard with eight views (Traveller's palm; Malay lady; Cavenagh Bridge; the Esplanade; Collyer Quay, a rickshaw; Johnston's Pier and an Indian lady) with decorative spiking palm leaves and flowers.

[492]
GREETINGS FROM SINGAPORE. (1899)

Cancellation: 1899
Back: Undivided
Publisher: G.R. Lambert & Co., Singapore

This is a colour-tinted postcard with eight views (Traveller's palm; Johnston's Pier; Cavenagh Bridge, Raffles Institution Battery Road; St. Andrew's Cathedral; a Chinese Tiffin House and a young Malay man).

[493]

SINGAPORE. SCENES IN KAMPONG BAHRU.
(1898)

Back: Undivided
Series and/or No.: 546
Publisher: Kunzli Frefres, Zurich

The scene in Kampong Bahru depicts the stilt
houses of the Orang Laut and three rickshaws in
the other view; the scene is framed by several
trees and shrubs.

[494]

SINGAPORE. ROADS WITH MARKETHALL. (1898)

Back: Undivided
Series and/or No.: 599
Publisher: Kunzli Frefres, Zurich

Shows the roads to Markethall and a rickshaw
with its puller and his two passengers. Behind
the rickshaw is a thick jungle; the view is framed
by a rectangular vignette.

PHILATELIC ASPECTS

Uncommon handstamps like "Late Fee Paid" can enhance the value of a postcard.
(*See* [496])

The addressee on a postcard can also enhance its value. This postcard was sent from Kelantan in 1905 to Southseas, England via Singapore. The Siamese stamps were cancelled in Singapore.
(*See* [497])

Philatelic Aspects of Picture Postcards

A picture postcard (ppc) has two sides: the picture side and the address side. To collectors of ppcs (cartologist, deltiologist or cartophilist), the picture side is more important. However, collectors of stamps and postal history (philatelists) consider the address side to be more important, for the stamp(s) or cancellation(s) details, and dates on a ppc can enhance its value considerably.

Among other factors, the value of a postcard is determined by the type and rates of stamps used, its cancellation dates and routes taken. Indeed, any serious collector should first scrutinise the address side of a ppc for any uncommon philatelic findings. It is not possible to discuss all the details of postal history of ppcs in this book, but a few pointers are listed below:

(A) The first Picture Postcard was made from a Postal Stationery Postcard

It is still possible to find such a ppc at a ppc fair. It is worth considerably more than the same picture on an ordinary ppc, so it is worthwhile to look for a postal stationery ppc!

(B) Stamp on Address Side or Picture Side

Most ppcs bear stamps on the address side (as it is intended to be) but some collectors prefer ppcs with stamps on the picture side. Since the early 1900s, collectors have requested for ppcs to be sent to them with the stamps on the picture side; hence such ppcs are common as shown in many of the ppcs in this book.

(C) Uncommon Destination

Uncommon destinations are more common in ppcs than in commercial letters. For example, a ppc sent to San Miguel in the Azores Islands is worth a small premium.

(D) Uncommon Cancellation/Hand Stamp

One of the most uncommon cancellations found on a ppc is that of the Sea View Hotel. [495] shows a ppc (Native Cooly, Singapore) sent from Singapore to England; it is franked with a 3¢ Straits Settlement stamp and the stamp is tied with the circular datestamp "SEA VIEW HOTEL/31 AU/1917/SINGAPORE". It has a further datestamp of Singapore with the same date. The Sea View Hotel had a post office in its premise from about 1915 to 1920. Raffles Hotel also had a post office from about 1910 to 1929. However, Raffles Hotel cancellations on ppcs are relatively common compared to that of the Sea View Hotel.

Another uncommon handstamp (instruction mark) on a ppc is shown [496 (*left, top*)]. The ppc was sent from Singapore to Ceylon; it was franked by a George V 4¢ and 10¢ stamp and cancelled by the circular datestamp of Singapore "MY 22/1922". It was carried by the steamer S.S. "Plassy" (written above the stamps); it was too late to be loaded on the ship by the regular launch and so it had to pay a late fee. The instruction mark "LATE FEE PAID" within a rectangular box was stamped prominently across the stamps.

(E) Uncommon Stamp/Label

The addressee on a ppc or cover can enhance its postal history interest. A ppc [497 (*left, middle*)] was sent by Dr. Gimlette in 1905 to his sister in Southsea, England. At that time, the Kelantan postal system was run by the Siamese post office; hence Siamese stamps were used. The ppc (Singapore, Suburban, Police Station) was sent via Singapore to England. It travelled to Singapore either by rail or coastal steamer. At Singapore, the 2 and 4 attangs stamps were cancelled and the ppc was carried to England by ship.

Labuan stamps overprinted "STRAITS SETTLEMENTS" were in use for a short period (1906–1907); such stamps used on commercial mail are scarce. A ppc franked with such a stamp (4¢ on 16¢) is shown [498 (*right, top*)].

In 1916, semi-official charity labels were issued for use on mail to raise funds for the welfare of British Servicemen fighting in the First World War. It was an additional payment on top of the usual postal rate. For example, [499 (*right, middle*)] shows a ppc sent from Singapore to Gopeng (Perak, Malaya); it was franked with the George V 1¢ green postage stamp. In addition it was also franked with a green 20¢ "Lord Roberts/Memorial Workshops" charity label. This charity label is rarely used on picture postcards or letters.

In 1922, the Malaya Borneo Exhibition was held in Singapore; the Straits Settlement stamps were overprinted for the Exhibition. [500] shows a ppc sent from Singapore to Scotland franked with a 4¢ stamp overprinted "MALAYA/ BORNEO /EXHIBITION". Ppcs bearing such an overprinted stamp are rare.

Valuation of Picture Postcards

Ppcs of Singapore from the prewar era (1897–1941) as covered in this book are worth from a few to over a thousand dollars. The value of a ppc can be determined by:

(A) Age

In general, the older a ppc is, the more valuable it is. For example, the first ppcs of Singapore that were made from the Straits Settlements 3¢ carmine on buff postal stationery postcard are highly prized among collectors.

(B) Rarity

Rare recent ppcs may be worth more than older but more common ppcs.

(C) Condition

The condition of a ppc is important in determining its value; damaged cards are seldom worth collecting. Blemishes such as creasing, rounded or folded corners, toning or foxing, faded colours, worm or spike holes diminish considerably the value of a ppc.

(D) Colouring

Colour pccs are more valuable than black and white ones. However, earlier hand-tinted coloured ppcs are worth more than the recent ones printed in colour.

(E) Used/unused postcards

Unused postcards are more common than those that have been used postally. However, used ppcs with stamps ripped off may be worth less than unused ppcs. As explained earlier, postal markings on a ppc can increase its value considerably.

A "Delightful Mess"

To a philatelist (or postal historian), the address side of the ppc is important – the more datestamps, obliterators, instructional handstamps, registration marks, retour marks there are, the more precious the ppc is to the collector. Indeed, all of the above present on the address side of a ppc would be regarded as a "delightful mess" to any philatelist!

Conclusion

How many different ppcs of Singapore were published from 1897 to 1941? No one knows for sure; a wild estimate would be about 2,000. However, the advent of the Internet and online auctions has rejuvenated the hobby of ppc collecting. Indeed, these new technologies have enabled ppc collectors to acquire rare and unusual ppcs from all around the world, and this has livened up the hobby of ppc collecting.

Labuan stamps overprinted "STRAITS SETTLEMENTS" used on commercial mail are scarce.
(*See* [498])

Semi-official charity labels were issued to aid the welfare of British Servicemen fighting in the First World War.
(*See* [499])

[495]
Untitled [Uncommon Cancellation].
Cancellation: 1917

Sent from Singapore to England in 1917, this
postcard is franked with a S.S. 3¢ King George V
stamp; the stamp is tied with the double-ring
circular date stamp "SEA VIEW HOTEL/31
AU/1917/SINGAPORE". The postcard was sent to
the General Post Office where it was further
cancelled on the same day (Sea View Hotel
cancellation is rare on postcards or letters).

[496]
Untitled [Hand Stamp].
Cancellation: 1922

This postcard was posted late and had to pay a
late fee to be rushed to the "S.S. Plassy" (written
above the stamps) by special launch. The two
King George V stamps (4¢ and 10¢) were tied by
the Singapore datestamp of 22 May 1922; over
the stamps were stamped prominently in black
"LATE FEE PAID" within a rectangular box.

[497]
Untitled [Uncommon Stamp/Label].

Cancellation: 1905

A "Gimlette" postcard sent from Kelantan via Singapore to Southsea, England. At that time Kelantan used Siamese stamps. This postcard was carried to Singapore by rail or steamer; the stamps were cancelled in Singapore and the postcard was then sent to England by sea.

[498]
Untitled [Uncommon Stamp].

Cancellation: 1907

A postcard franked with the 4¢ on 16¢ Labuan stamp overprinted "STRAITS SETTLEMENTS". The stamp is tied by the circular datestamp "SINGAPORE/JA 7/1907"; this stamp is seldom found used on a postcard as it was in use for only a short period (1906–1907).

[499]
Untitled [Uncommon Label].

Cancellation: 1916

Semi-official charity labels were issued to aid the welfare of British Servicemen fighting in the First World War. Such a label, a green 20¢ "Lord Roberts/Memorial Workshops/Straits Settlements/War Fund" label was used together with a 1¢ stamp on this postcard.

Raffles Hotel, Singapore.   No. 5

[500]
Untitled [Overprinted Stamp].

Cancellation: 1924

A postcard sent from Singapore to Scotland and franked with a 4¢ S.S. stamp overprinted "MALAYA/BORNEO/EXHIBITION". Such a stamp used on a postcard is rare.

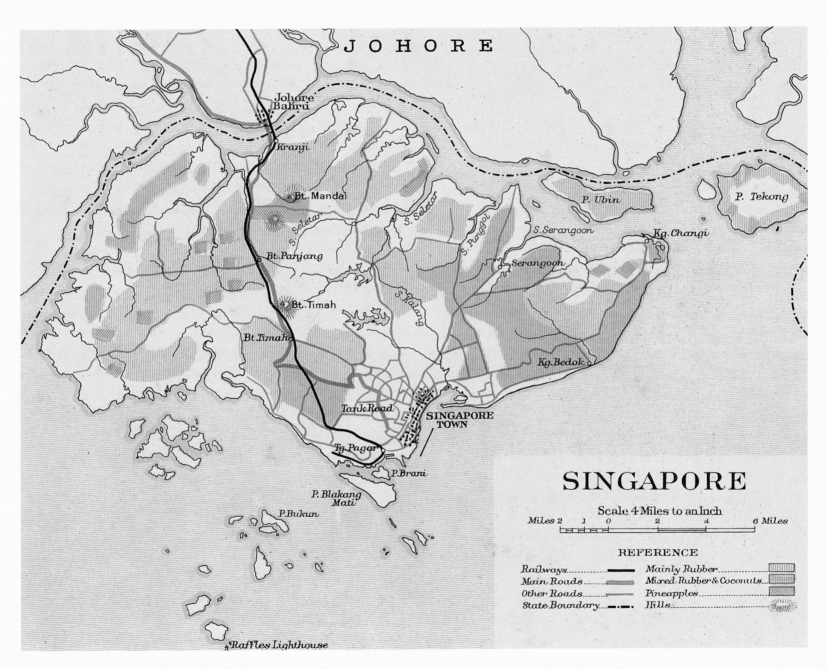

JOHORE

Johore Bahru

Kranji

Bt. Mandai

S. Seletar

S. Seletar

Bt. Panjang

S. Punggol

P. Ubin

S. Serangoon

Kg. Changi

P. Tekong

Serangoon

S. Selang

Bt. Timah

Kg. Bedok

Bt. Timah

Tank Road

SINGAPORE
TOWN

Tg. Pagar

P. Brani

P. Blakang
Mati

P. Bukun

SINGAPORE

Scale 4 Miles to an Inch

Miles 2 1 0 2 4 6 Miles

REFERENCE

Railways	Mainly Rubber
Main Roads	Mixed Rubber & Coconuts
Other Roads	Pineapples
State Boundary	Hills

Raffles Lighthouse

ACKNOWLEDGEMENTS

I would like to extend my heartfelt thanks to :

- Mr. Timothy Auger, Miss Laura Gobal, Mr. Gregory Lee and the team at Editions Didier Millet for making this book possible.
- Mr. Peter How Kian Huat for technical help.
- My fellow collectors for useful information: Mr. Alan Au Yong, Dr. Chua Eu Tiong, Mr. Hong Tuck Kung, Mr. Koh Kim Chay, Mr. Lim Kheng Chye, Mr. Ong Bok Lim, Mr. Richard Thio, Dr. Toh Kok Thye and Mr. Wong Han Min.
- Miss Nancy Woong for secretarial help.

ABOUT THE AUTHOR

Professor Cheah Jin Seng is an avid philatelist and deltiologist, and is particularly well-versed in the postal history of Singapore and Malaysia. Born in Penang, he is currently a Fellow of the Royal Philatelic Society of London and a Director of the Singapore Philatelic Museum. An ex-board member of the Singapore History Museum, Prof. Cheah has also written and co-published extensively on the subjects of stamps and postcards in Singapore and Malaysia.

Prof. Cheah also collects Peranakan artifacts, old photographs and books pertaining to the medical and local history of Singapore, Malaysia and the Straits Settlements.

By profession, Prof. Cheah is a Physician and an Endocrinologist, having obtained his Bachelor of Medicine and Surgery (Honours) and a Doctorate of Medicine from the National University of Singapore. He is also a Fellow of the following institutions: the Royal Australasian College of Physicians, the Royal College of Physicians, Edinburgh, and the Academy of Medicine, Singapore.

A.....

J. **Aberle**, Berlin

Aulard, Iung et Cie, Paris

B.....

J. **Beagles** & Co. Ltd., England

J. **Brignon**

C.....

The **Continental Stamp Company**, Singapore

Court i and B.A, Haase, Prague

D.....

A.M. **Davis** & Co., London

Thomas **De La Rue** Co., London

F.....

Kunzli **Freres**, Zurich

G.....

Gale & Polden, Ltd, Aldershot

Devambez, **Grav**, Editeur, France

H.....

Haase P.A., Prague

Hartwig & Co. Succ., Singapore

Imp. **Hermieu**, Paris

Max H. **Hilckes**, Singapore

K.P. **Hock**, Singapore

Houghton Butcher (Eastern) Ltd., "Camera House", Robinson
    Road, Singapore

J.....

Johs, Krogers, Buchdruckere I., Blan-Keneye, N., Hamburg,
    Germany

K.....

Kelly & Walsh Ltd, Singapore

G.H. **Kiat** & Co. Ltd, Singapore

C.J. **Kleingrothe**, Medan

Koh & Co., Singapore

Kong Hing Chiong & Co., North Bridge Road, Singapore

L.....

Lim Swee Yak, Singapore

John **Little** & Co. Ltd, Singapore

G.R. **Lambert** and Co., Singapore

Max **Ludwig**, Deutsche Buchhandlung, Singapore

Ludwig & Ressel's Reisebuchanallung, Singapore

M.....

Manicum S.M., Singapore

Methodist Publishing House, Singapore

M.J., Penang

M.W.P., Singapore

N.....

M.S. **Nakajima**, Singapore

P.....

Pattara Z.

R.....

C.A. **Ribeiro** & Co., Singapore

S.....

Stengel & Co., Dresden u, Berlin

T.....

Raphael **Tuck** & Sons, London

W.....

Photogravure, **Waterlow** & Sons Limited, London

Whiteaway Laidlaw & Co., Singapore

Wilson & Co. Photographers, Orchard Road, Singapore

Y.....

Mohamed **Yahya**, Singapore

Above: CHILDREN OF THE EMPIRE. (C 1930)
Back: Divided
Series and/or No.: 577
Publisher: A.M. Davis & Co., London

FURTHER READING

1. Staff, Frank. *The Picture Postcard and its Origins* London: Lutterworth Press, 1966.

2. Ministry of Culture, Singapore. *Singapore 1870s–1940s in Pictures* Singapore: Koon Wah Lithographers, 1980.

3. Sin Chew Jit Poh and Ministry of Culture. *Singapore in Pictures* Singapore: Sin Chew Jit Poh, 1981.

4. Sin Chew Jit Poh and Archives and Oral History Department. *Singapore Retrospect Through Postcards: 1900–1930* Singapore: Sin Chew Jit Poh, 1982.

5. Liu, Gretchen, ed. *Singapore Historical Postcards from the National Archive Collection* Singapore: Times Editions, 1986.

6. Mialaret, Jean-Pierre. *Passing Through Singapore, 1900–1930* Singapore: Graham Brash, 1986.

7. National Archives of Malaysia and National Archives of Singapore. *Reminiscences of the Straits Settlements Through Postcards* Ed. Lee Geok Boi. Singapore/Kuala Lumpur: KHL Printing Co. Ltd, 2005.

8. Doggett, Marjorie. *Characters of Light: A Guide to the Buildings of Singapore* Singapore: Donald Moore, 1957.

9. Tyres, Ray. *Singapore Then & Now* 2 vols. Singapore: University Education Press, 1976.

10. Haks, Leo, and Steven Wachlin. *Indonesia 500 Early Postcards* Singapore: Archipelago Press – Editions Didier Millet, 1986.

11. Mortimer, Chris. "A Postcard View of Old Singapore – early cards." *Asian Phonecards & Collectibles (Singapore)* 2 (1997): pp. 10–11.

12. Wong Han Min. "A Postcard View of Old Singapore – The Golden Age." *Asian Phonecards & Collectibles (Singapore)* 9 (1997): pp. 30–32.

13. Khoo, Salma Nasution, and Malcom Wade. *Penang: Postcard Collection 1899–1930s* Penang: Janus & Resources, 2003. p. 12.

14. Mortimer, Chris. "Singapore's privately printed picture postcards – the early history (Part I)." *Picture Postcard Monthly (UK)* 197 (Sept 1995): pp. 49–53.

15. Mortimer, Chris. "Singapore's privately printed picture postcards – the early history (Part 2)." *Picture Postcard Monthly (UK)* 205 (May 1996): pp. 16–19.

16. Wong Han Min. "A Postcard View of Old Singapore – The Early Cards." *Asian Phonecards & Collectibles (Singapore)* 8 (1996): pp. 30–32.

17. Falconer, John. *A vision of the past: A history of early photography in Singapore and Malaya. The photographs of G.R. Lambert & Co, 1880–1910* Singapore: Times Editions, 1987.

18. Wright, Arnold, and H.A. Cartwright. *Twentieth Century Impressions of British Malaya: its History, People, Commerce, Industries and Resources* London: Lloyd's Greater Britain Publishing Co. Ltd, 1908.

19. *Postcard Exchange Register/A Monthly Journal* 2.13 Singapore: Koh & Co., 1908.

20. *Postcard Exchange Register/A Monthly Journal* 3.21 Singapore: Koh & Co., 1909.

21. *Postcard Exchange Register/A Monthly Journal* 3.17 Singapore: Koh & Co., 1909.

22. Higgins & Cage Incorporated. *Priced Catalogue of Postal Stationery of the World* Pasadena, California, USA: Lamanda Park Printing & Litho Co., 1971.

23. Wong Han Min. *A Postcard View of Old Singapore – The Early Cards. Asian Phonecards and Collectibles (Singapore)* 1.2 (1995): p. 30.

24. Bailey Co. Ltd. *A Collection of 19th Century Postcards of Singapore by G.R. Lambert* Singapore: Bailey Co. Pte Ltd, not dated (c 1990).

25. Tanzer, Marlene, ed. *Singapore Lifeline – The River and its People* Singapore: Times Books International in conjunction with the Archives and Oral History Department, 1986.

26. Berry, Linda. *Singapore's River – A Living Legacy* Singapore: Eastern Universities Press Sdn Bhd, 1982.

27. Liu, Gretchen. *Singapore: A Pictorial History 1819 – 2000* Singapore: Archipelago Press, 1999. p. 57.

28. Yap, Chris. *A Port's Story: A Nation's Success* Singapore: Kim Hup Lee Printing Co. Pte Ltd, 1990.

29. Makepeace, Brooke Gilbert E., and Roland St. J. Braddell, eds. *One Hundred Years of Singapore* 2 vols. London: John Murray, 1921.

30. Lee, Edwin. *Historic Buildings of Singapore* Singapore: Singapore: National Printers, 1990.

31. Pugalenthi, Sr. *A Stroll Through Old Singapore: Esplanade* Singapore: V J Times, 1993.

32. Savage, Victor R., and Brenda Yeoh. *Toponymics: A Study of Singapore Street Names*. Singapore: Eastern Universities Press, 2003.

33. Song Ong Siang. *One Hundred Years' History of the Chinese in Singapore* London: John Murray, 1923.

34. *The Singapore and Straits Directory* 37th ed. Singapore: Fraser & Neave Ltd, 1916.

35. Koh Kim Chay. Personal Communication. 2005.

36. Koh Kim Chay. "Bank Blanda." *Singapore Stamp Club Newsletter* Apr 2002.

37. Richard Thio. Personal Communications. 2005.

38. *Chinatown: An Album of a Singapore Community* Singapore: Times Books International/Archives and Oral History Department, 1983.

39. Lip, Evelyn. *Chinese Temple Architecture in Singapore* Singapore: Singapore University Press, 1983.

40. Comber, Leon. *Chinese Temples in Singapore* Singapore: Malaya Publishing House Ltd, 1958.

41. Cheah Jin Seng. "Opium Addiction in Penang and British Malaya (1786–1941)" Rpt. in *To Heal The Sick* Ed. Ong Hean Teik. Penang: The Phoenix Press, 2004.

42. Koh Kim Chay. "The Straits Chinese Recreation Club." *Singapore Stamp Club Newsletter* Sep/Dec 2002.

43. Haw Par Brothers International Ltd. *Legend from a Jar: The Story of Haw Par. 25th Anniversary Commemorative Book* Singapore: Su Yeang Design Pte Ltd, 1994.

44. Cheah Jin Seng, and Ng Beng Yeong. "Centenary of the Faculty of Medicine and the National University of Singapore (1905–2005)." *Annals of the Academy of Medicine, Singapore* 34.6 (Jul 2005): pp. 1-3.

45. Vickers, W.J. *Annual Report of the Medical Department, Colony of Singapore* Singapore: Government Printing Office, 1946. p. 30.

46. Heritage Committee of the Japanese Association Singapore. *Prewar Japanese Community in Singapore – Picture and Record* Singapore: Kyodo Printing Co. (S) Pte Ltd, 1998.

47. *The Singapore Artillery – 100th Year Commemorative Book* Singapore: Stamford Press Pte Ltd, 1988.

48. Koh Kim Chay. "The Chinese Gospel Hall." *Singapore Stamp Club Newsletter* Mar 2004.

49. Crawley, Ray. *The Union Jack Club.* 19 Oct 2005. <http://www.britains-smallwars.com/Museum/Malaya/UJc.html>.

50. Flower, Raymond. *Raffles/The Story of Singapore* Singapore: Singapore National Printers (Pte) Ltd, 1984.

51. Quah, Yvonne. *We Remember/Cameos of Pioneer Life* Singapore: Landmark Books Pte Ltd, 1986.

52. *St. Anthony's Canossian Secondary School – School Information* 19 Oct 2005. <http://www.schoolsmoe.edu.sg/sac/history.htm>.

53. National Heritage Board. *Singapore's 100 Historic Places* Singapore: Archipelago Press, 2002.

54. *Victoria School (Singapore)* 19 Oct 2005. <http://www.en.wikipedia. org/wiki/Victoria_school>.

55. *Anglo-Chinese School* 19 Oct 2005. <http://www.en.wikipedia. org/wiki/Anglo_Chinese_School>.

56. Collins, W.L. *Directory of Commerce, Retailers & Residents (Straits Settlements)* Singapore: The Far East Publishing Syndicate, 1935.

57. *Young Women's Christian Association (1875–1995)* Singapore: Amour Publishing Pte Ltd, 1995.

58. Lee Kip Lin. *The Singapore House: 1819–1942* Singapore: Times Editions, 1988.

59. *Oldham Hall* 19 Oct 2005. <http://www.oldhamhall.org/abt_hist.htm>.

60. Lyne, Roland, C. Gopal Mennon, Edward Ong, and Ong Ai Teik. *The YMCA of Singapore/90 Years of Service to the Community* Singapore: Stamford Press Ltd, 1992.

61. *The Presbyterian Church in Singapore* 19 Oct 2005 <http://www.presbyterian.org.sg/1/index.jsp>.

62. Seet K.K. *The Istana* Singapore: Times Editions, 2000.

63. Siddique, Sharon, and Nirmala Shotam-gove, eds. *Serangoon Road/A Pictorial History* Singapore: Educational Publications Bureau Pte Ltd, 1983.

64. Choppard, K. *Rochore/Eyewitness* Singapore: Landmark Books Pte Ltd, 1989.

65. Koh Kim Chay. "Bidadari Christian Cemetry." *Singapore Stamp Club Newsletter* Jan 2002.

66. *Bukit Timah Nature Reserve* 1 Nov 2005. <http://www.nparks.gov.sg/nparks>.

67. National Archives of Singapore. *A Visual Documentation of Geylang Serai – Down Memory Lane* Singapore: Heinemann Publishers Asia Pte Ltd, 1986.

68. *Singapore Swimming Club* 5 Nov 2005. <http://www.sswimclub.org.sg/ milestones.asp>.

69. Au Yong, Alan. "The Brothers' Bungalow" *The Malayan Philatelist (UK)* 44.1 London: The Malaya Study Group, 2003. p. 10.

70. *Demographics of Singapore* 8 Nov 2005. <http://www.en.wikipedia.org/wiki/Demographics_of_Singapore>

71. Buckley, C.B. *An Anecdotal History of Old Times in Singapore, 1819–1867* Singapore: Fraser & Neave, 1902.

72. Khoo Joo Ee. *The Straits Chinese: A Cultural History* Amsterdam/Kuala Lumpur: The Pepin Press, 1996.

73. Cheah Jin Seng. *Porcelain with topographic scenes of Penang – an unrecognised category of Nonya Ware. Penang: Past & Present* Penang: Island Printers Sdn. Bhd, 1999.

74. Archives and Oral History Department. *Singapore: The Land Transport of Singapore/from early times to the present* Singapore: Education Publications Bureau Pte Ltd, 1984.

75. Archives and Oral History Department Singapore. *Singapore Fly-Past/A pictorial history of civil aviation in Singapore 1911–1981* Singapore: MPH Magazines (S) Pte Ltd, 1982.

76. *Visit of His Royal Highness the Prince of Wales/Details of Arrangements/Singapore/31st March – 1st April 1922* Singapore: Government Printers, 1922.

77. *Public Celebrations in honour of the Silver Jubilee of His Majesty King George V/6th May/1935* Singapore: Printers Limited, 1935.

78. Knight, Donlad R., and Alan D. Sabey. *The Lion roars at Wembley* London: Barhand & Westwoods Limited, 1984.